Pop Culture Literacies

This book illustrates how young people engage with pop culture—music, TV, films, fashion, dance, video games, memes, and digital content in its many forms—and outlines lessons that support them in engaging more actively, critically, and strategically.

Part One draws on qualitative research with young people, as well as close analyses of pop culture phenomena, to illustrate how young people already engage with pop culture, on- and offline. This research demonstrates that young people interpret and respond to pop culture texts in sophisticated ways and highlights the potential for supporting and challenging them to do so in ways that are even more active, critical, and strategic.

Part Two presents lessons that teach young people how to adopt intentional interpretive stances in relation to pop culture texts, identify and analyze hidden layers of story in these texts, and ultimately expand and refine their interpretations and responses. In the final chapter's lessons, young people engage in a process of developing a multimodal autoethnography, a form of narrative composition that explores the connections between the personal and the cultural. The book provides options for teaching these lessons as standalone lessons, for enmeshing them in standards-aligned humanities curricula, and for teaching them in sequence as a unit of study.

This book is ideal for teachers who want to better understand how their students are engaging in and making sense of the pop culture texts that saturate the digital world and to help them reimagine who they are in and out of that world.

Mia Hood is a curriculum designer, writing coach, and teacher educator based in New York. She has worked as a professor of literacy and secondary education at the City University of New York and a professor of professional writing at New York University. Mia received her doctorate in Curriculum and Teaching from Teachers College, where she studied sociocultural and critical perspectives on literacy.

Pop Culture Literacies

Teaching Interpretation, Response, and
Composition in a Digital World

Mia Hood

Routledge
Taylor & Francis Group
NEW YORK AND LONDON

First published 2025
by Routledge
605 Third Avenue, New York, NY 10158

and by Routledge
4 Park Square, Milton Park, Abingdon, Oxon, OX14 4RN

Routledge is an imprint of the Taylor & Francis Group, an informa business

ISBN: 978-1-032-66611-2 (hbk)
ISBN: 978-1-032-66704-1 (pbk)
ISBN: 978-1-032-66702-7 (ebk)

DOI: 10.4324/9781032667027

Typeset in Palatino
by Apex CoVantage, LLC

Dedication

For Harper, Luca, and Perrine

And for my honorary niblings, near and far

Contents

Meet the Author

Mia Hood is a lifelong reader, writer, and teacher of reading, writing, and teaching. Across two decades in education, Mia has served in a variety of K-12 roles, including classroom teacher, instructional dean, and, most recently, director of literacy for a network of schools in New York City. Currently, she designs curriculum for schools and nonprofits, coaches writers, and teaches literacy and secondary education at the City University of New York and professional writing at New York University. Mia received her doctorate in Curriculum and Teaching from Teachers College, Columbia University, where she studied sociocultural and critical perspectives on literacy. She has written about curriculum, teaching, and literacy for *Education Week*, *HuffPost*, the *Journal for Multicultural Education*, Sesame Workshop, and Heinemann. She's presented her scholarly work at conferences of the International Literacy Association, Literacy Research Association, and American Educational Studies Association. She writes all about pop culture literacies in the newsletter Popstack.

Acknowledgments

I must begin by acknowledging and thanking the two people who were right there with me over this project's many years: Sherry Deckman and Tran Nguyen Templeton. In the early days of the pandemic, Sherry was there as I roamed Central Park, talking me through every last glimmer of a whim of a notion of an idea about pop culture and answering my every question about writing a book (my every question several times over, she'd point out). She read the first chapter I drafted in a very early, just barely serviceable form and told me, in so many words, what I needed to hear: keep going.

Tran was there every Sunday morning, in her preferred coffee shop or mine, capitulating to my demands that she explain memes and sundry artifacts of digital culture to me. She also sent me helpful TikTok after helpful TikTok, material I'd only discover months later and too late, after a period of refusing to open the app. Tran encouraged me as only she can: through careful observation and loving scrutiny of my every last move.

I am, of course, understating Sherry's and Tran's contributions to this work—doomed to do so, I'd say, given how tightly I've knitted my own thinking into theirs, how many of my own ideas, I'm convinced, were actually their ideas first. Their wisdom is, if not indistinguishable from, foundational to my understanding of the world.

Marjorie Siegel and Dani Friedrich supported this work at its earliest stages, when it was a dissertation with way too many disparate parts, held together only by my obstinacy. By their guidance and by the example of their own work, they helped me see pop culture as an intellectually worthy object of study. And they always nudged me to look again, to think again, to not let any of the juicy bits of a pop culture text go unexamined or unconsumed.

In the early days of research, the faculty of Horizon Middle helped me identify the pop culture enthusiasts among their students, gathered them for me when they were drawn to more enticing after-school activities, gave up their classroom space, and kept helping me get the projector to work. It was ever a delight to detect evidence of their superb teaching in the girls' pop culture interpretations. Clearly, their students were already being nurtured to be the active, critical, and strategic readers and writers we want them to be. And, of course, this project would not have been possible without Audrey, Briana, Danielle, Jasmine, and Kaylee. All they had to be was game, but, as it turned out, they were also insightful, warm, silly, wise, witty, and fun. I hope they'll always look back on that random after-school club they did with that random researcher-lady with the fondness I do.

I thank the multihyphenates in my life—the educator-scholar-colleague-friends—who championed this work. Chantal Francois, writing her own book as I wrote mine, advised me to work on it a little bit every day rather than as I was inclined to do it: once a week for 16 hours straight gripped by panic. I mostly ignored this sage advice, but I thank Chantal nevertheless for always making the impossible seem possible, bit by bit. I thank those who've shaped me as an educator top to bottom, inside out. Wendy Colmus, Ugochi Emenaha, Jessica Hahn, Megan Morgalis, Lucy Patranella, Sayuri Stabrowski, and Candace Sharrow gave me invaluable insider feedback on the lessons in the second half of this book, but they all had a hand in shaping my pedagogy long before that. Kimberly Austin came through, as she's known to do, with critical insights about how identity shapes and is shaped by digital engagement.

If it weren't for the many friends and loved ones who expanded my pop culture repertoire, this book would have been entirely about elder Millennial fashion and late 90s comfort TV. My brother Sloan Hood helped me conceptualize and taxonomize video game genres, checking my understanding and my adjectives. Like father like daughter, Harper Hood added to my understanding of the live-stream chat and extended my menu of character-driven memes. Claire Fridkin, in both dinner party chitchat and comments in the doc, refined my understanding of the semiosis of memes and influencer content. And I've learned much about the possibility of critical engagement with pop culture texts, whether of the *Sex and the City* or the *Love is Blind* variety, from Stephanie Salazar's example and our digital repartee.

I owe thanks to Sarah Tuttle and Ben Gummoe, without whom this book would have never contained references to livestock learning viral dances and promotional popcorn buckets that resemble genitalia. I'm grateful to them for brainstorming with me and for their courtesy in not pointing out that I perhaps should have been at home writing, rather than sipping wine with them in the Finger Lakes. From Eric Sanderson, I learned the ins and outs of music production, and from Caitlin Rain, how cultural and sociohistorical contexts shape fashion. Eric and Caitlin helped me sound much fancier than I am in my descriptions of pop music and fashion memes, respectively. On a beach in Aruba, Rachel Fairbanks, narrative savant that she is, paused her otherwise incessant sunscreen reapplication to offer, off the top of her head, half a dozen short film examples for Chapter 5, recapitulating every plot point in meticulous detail at a length that doubled the runtime of the films themselves. And, finally, wide-ranging, reflective conversations—the very best kind!—with Caitlin Müschenborn and Jamie Axelrod helped me re-evaluate the impact of digital culture on children and young people.

So many young people have sharpened my understanding of pop culture engagement. Luca Hood let me watch him play *Fortnite* and let me in on the lingo. My semi-annual slumber parties with Perrine Hood have always been a real education for me. She's shown me how to hold two contrasting truths in one hand: that, for example, even if digital content is brain poison, it's also just so undeniably intriguing. I have my young friend Cate to thank for finally, and officially, initiating me into Swiftiedom by teaching me how to make friendship bracelets. I'm indebted to Rowan and Remy for their generosity in answering my many questions about what they do on their devices and why they do it. Anijah Lucena educated me about the practice of watching entire films in clips on TikTok and introduced me to the term

"Millennial pause," both of which clarified for me the distinctions between how Millennials and Gen Z engage with social media. And, finally, I thank my students at Thrive Academy—especially Aarmeen, Alison, Chelsea, Cindy, Dennis, Frida, Kaylin, Laura, Mena, Winlly, and Youngna—who stuck around after class in the final weeks to teach me about VTubers, dark TikTok, and the virtues of crew socks.

Lastly, I thank those who have always held my spirits and my ambitions aloft: my parents, the inimitable Janice and Bob Hood; my siblings by birth and marriage, Sloan, Rachel, Zach, and Ashley (Hoods, all); and the friends named above, as well as Amanda Addison, Steve Colmus, Sunjay Dixit, Chelsea Egner, Diana Halluska, and Claudia Soriano. They supported me by asking how the book was going either all the time or none of the time—nothing in between—and by being, in either case, quick to toast my every accomplishment and sub-accomplishment along the way. And I owe special thanks to Erin Trieb who, in the 24 hours leading up to this book's deadline, as I suggested one fun social outing after the next, gently reminded me that it would also be okay if I needed to just sit on her couch and finish the conclusion.

I'm profoundly grateful to have had the opportunity to write the book of my dreams. I did so in the interstices of the much larger project of my day jobs: teaching teachers and designing curriculum. In the moment, I didn't feel especially grateful to be doing so much all at once, but, from this vantage point, I can appreciate the interplay of teaching, designing, and writing: how each activity undoes but somehow ultimately enhances the others. Those I've named here, and many I haven't, helped me make sense of how these pieces of my work—and, in fact, my life—sometimes fit together and sometimes don't. I'm grateful to live my life among them, to sit beside them, deconstructing and reconstructing our understandings and experiences of the complicated world we inhabit.

Introduction

In November 2002, the music video for Jennifer Lopez's single "Jenny from the Block" premiered on MTV's *Total Request Live*. In the video, paparazzi shots misrepresent mundane activities. Lopez has something caught in her eye, but, in the shot, she appears to be crying. Affleck kneels to hand Lopez an earring she'd dropped, but, in the shot, he appears to be proposing. The song's lyrics and the video are, ostensibly, Lopez's attempt to reclaim "realness," which, in the video's account, has been threatened by the intrusive mediation of the telephoto lens. Despite her fame and wealth, she's still, she insists, "Jenny from the block."

According to the logic of the video, it is the camera that distorts the reality of her lived experience, creating a chasm between what she experiences and what we, her "public," see. The *real*, in this configuration, is purer and nobler than the flattened image we consume. According to the lyrics, we can be assured that Lopez is real because she has "been on Oprah." In her attempt to reclaim realness, the meaning of *realness* is deferred to yet another mediated (and, obviously, not very relatable) experience of appearing on a popular TV show.

This analysis, plus or minus a few phrases, was written 20 years ago. I lifted it from my senior thesis, a piece of writing vulgar in its self-importance and prone to bold, unsupported claims like, "VH1 is the apotheosis of the televisual experience." It's an embarrassing affair, revisiting it, but it's also a snapshot that illuminates all that's changed about pop culture in the past two decades, and all that's stayed the same. The way the camera mediates and distorts human experience. The way the texture and idiosyncrasies of life are flattened into glossy images. The way narrative has subordinated itself to image and rhythm. The futile desire to reclaim *realness* from a cultural milieu of hyper-representation. This used to be Lopez's problem; now, it seems, it's ours.

DOI: 10.4324/9781032667027-1

This book is not about pop culture but about engagement with pop culture. It's about how we as educators can help young people orient themselves to a digital world awash in cultural commodities—how we might teach them to be self-aware and intentional about how they consume culture, so that culture doesn't consume them.

A Brief History of Pop Culture

Writing about pop culture is like trying to hold on to a water wiggler toy. As soon as you fix your grip, it slips from your hand. Pop culture is always slipping out of the hands of those who try to describe it. Its transformation is perpetual because the trans-formation of the technologies that enable its production, distri-bution, and consumption is likewise perpetual.

Still, when I read the pop culture scholarship of the late 20th century, I can't help but notice that the concepts and descriptive frameworks of then apply today. Whole sentences and paragraphs hold, if we swap out some nouns and verbs, Mad Lib-style. Back then, it was the proliferation of cable TV channels and the practice of flipping through them that flattened content, elevating commercial junk and burying the good stuff. Today, it's the social media feed. Back then, it was the Minimoog synthesizer that removed the human hand from the production of pop music. Today, it's the Moises app. Back then, it was random chance that produced the uncanny assemblages of content we consumed. Today, it's an algo-rithm. What I hope to do in this book is find a way to help young people orient themselves to the culture they inhabit. Underlying the major inquiry is a question of how culture changes, and how it stays the same.

I begin with a statement of where we are, however incom-plete it may be, and a retracing of how we got here. In the brief history of pop culture that follows, we'll look at how culture has fragmented and become less communal and more customized.

Mass culture emerged in the 1920s when new technologies—radio broadcasting, motion pictures, phonographs—made

cultural products widely accessible, and the availability of consumer goods—cars, ready-to-wear clothes, electric appliances—
gave Americans more leisure time to enjoy them (Storey, 2021).
Over the next 50 years, most notably when television manufacturing took off post-war, culture pushed its way into our homes.
By the time I was growing up in the 1980s and 90s, mass culture
had changed, yes, but it was still a monoculture (Wu, 2016). The
culture industries supplied us with a relatively small set of TV
shows, movies, fashion styles, sporting events, and music to
consume. At that time, aspiring writers, directors, actors, musical
artists, and others had to rely on the apparatuses of the three
major TV networks and a small set of film studios and record
companies to create and distribute their work.

Then, in the early 90s, the TV industry began to expand. By
the mid-90s, more than half of American households had cable
TV, exploding the menu of at-home viewing options (Federal
Communications Commission, 1996). The proliferation of
infrared remote controls meant that we didn't just not need to
leave our homes to consume culture, we didn't need to leave our
couches. TV was no longer a domestic analog of a movie theater: a coherent (if not necessarily aesthetically worthy) viewing
experience. Flipping channels fragmented the viewing experience. Bits and pieces of ideas, images, and information were
thrown together by chance and didn't amount to anything more
than what we made of it.

In some ways, the arrival of streaming services and the
concomitant swelling of the body of so-called prestige TV in
the 2010s could be seen as a detour from this lockstep march
toward total cultural fragmentation. As Reynolds (2019) notes,
everyday viewers had more power than ever before to curate
our viewing experiences and, in some circles, our careful curation came to index something deeper about our sociocultural
identities. That late 2010s feeling that we were at the dawn of a
new era of deep engagement with cultural products was only
enhanced by streaming platforms' autoplay features, which
encouraged binge-watching.

But, of course, the claim of deep engagement hinges on
what we mean by *deep*. It's true that viewers could, and often

did, consume entire seasons of TV in one big gulp. But we must remember that the streaming boom was preceded by the smartphone boom of the late aughts and early 2010s. With smartphones in our hands, we re-fragmented our own consumption habits, splitting our attention across the big screens in our living rooms and the little screens in our hands.

There's a parallel story to be told about how we consume popular music. In the 1920s, the gramophone was a common household item, its accessibility rising along with the rise of popular forms of dance and music genres like jazz, blues, and big band (Wu, 2016). Over the next 60 years, gramophones became record players, and record players became cassette players, and the experience of listening to music became more private, moving from dancehalls, to homes, to bedrooms, and eventually to headphones. In the early 1990s, I accessed—and curated—pop music by loading up my radio-cassette player with a blank tape, waiting for 106.1 KISS FM to play my song, and pressing record. The resulting mixtapes reflected my careful curation, but they were still a hodgepodge. I enjoyed my parents' oldies station as much as I enjoyed Top 40, so I'd have Martha and the Vandellas' (1964) "Dancing in the Street" alongside Tag Team's "Whoomp! (There It Is)" (1993). Such combinations, interspersed with the back-announce I'd accidentally pick up when I didn't stop the recording quickly enough, are still imprinted in my memory.

By the time I started college in 2000, my generation had gained near total control of our music consumption, thanks to Napster, the peer-to-peer file sharing app that enabled widespread distribution of mp3 audio files (Forde, 2019). Now able to download and listen to anything and everything, I was drawn to nostalgic songs that never did play on Top 40. In my early 20s, I got my hands on an iPod and, by the late aughts, I had every song on earth available to be piped directly into my ears with a few taps of a finger.

This has been the story of how, over the past century, pop culture moved from the moviehouse to our living rooms to our hands; from the dancehall to the bedroom to our hands. Our engagements with pop culture have become more fragmented, less communal, and more customized—customized by us, by an algorithm, and by the interplay between the two. There's an argument to be made that the culture industries have been democratized. Today, anyone with a smartphone can create and distribute content. Ideas, images, and information that were once the purview of only a few powerful people sitting atop film studios, record companies, and the like are now in nearly everyone's hands. In this way, today, pop culture is truly of the people.

It would be comforting to think that the fragmentation of culture could prove to be a powerful countervailing force to the rule of the rich and powerful few. But the thought strains credulity since the technologies we use to create and circulate digital content are developed, sold, and controlled by the rich and powerful few who sit atop tech companies. The content we swim in might look like free-floating particles but, when we tilt our heads and squint our eyes and look at them another way, they look like capital. We didn't necessarily ask for the technologies that fragmented culture. They were foisted upon us.

That brings us to AI's role in the culture industries. Given AI's nascency, it feels foolish at this point in time (late 2024) to make bold claims about what AI means or will mean, what it is doing or will do to society. I'll strive, then, not to be bold, but to be descriptive. To borrow the language of novelist and neuroscientist Erik Hoel (2024), AI is sludge in the cultural ocean, late capitalism's runoff now polluting everything from social media feeds to magazine articles to the peer review process.

In many ways, even beyond those Hoel (2024) describes, AI is our collective runoff: the runoff of the institutions we've built and the technologies through which we communicate and express ourselves. I think of AI's work in the cultural sphere as telling us back—and, in doing so, reifying—who we are, what we've become. By design, AI sweeps away the idiosyncrasies, variations, and ineffable complexities of human experience, normalizing particular ways of thinking, communicating, and interacting.

While our pop culture engagements are becoming more fragmented, less communal, and more customized, while we're pulling away from each other and burying ourselves in the algorithmically produced subcultures of our own devices (Chayka, 2024), AI is accelerating a movement in the opposite direction. All of the bits of content we've created are being aggregated into a singular intelligence, a singular way of making and expressing meaning.

The blessing of AI, as I see it, is that it makes what's already been happening at a structural level in American schools—the routinization and mechanization of teaching and learning (Unwin & Yandell, 2016)—more obvious. When I read pop culture scholarship of the late 20th century, I find terms that are useful in describing this moment. Baudrillard's (1981/1994) *simulacrum*, for example, or Fredric Jameson's (1991) *pastiche*. AI is both new and, thoroughly, nothing new.

What does it mean to be human in this context? How do we flourish in a world in which companies mine value from our attention (Lorenz, 2023)? How can we mount some resistance? I'd suggest there's a lot to learn from the ways in which young people are already doing so, engaging with and creating content in agentive, creative, strategic, and critical ways.

Overview of the Book

This book has two parts. The purpose of the first part is to propose a framework for understanding pop culture literacies, and the purpose of the second is to provide pop culture literacy lessons for adolescents and teens. Here, I offer some overarching definitions of recurring terms, provide background on the research from which this larger inquiry emerged, and prophylactically disclose three caveats, which, if I didn't get them off my chest here, would have littered the prose.

Definitions

Throughout the book, I'll refer to texts and *pop culture* texts, literacy and *pop culture* literacy. These definitions are, of course, interdependent. For my purposes, a **text** is any object, physical or digital, created by humans, directly or indirectly, that makes meaning available to others. In academic contexts, we often use *text* narrowly, to refer only to written language. Certainly, many of the texts discussed in this book will involve written language. But because language is not the only sign system through which meaning is constructed (Bezemer & Kress, 2003), and because multimodal texts dominate the digital spaces we inhabit, any relevant contemporary definition of *text* must be bigger than that. In my view, an episode of a TV show is a text, a song is a text, a video game is a text, a TikTok is a text, an article of clothing is a text, a toy is a text. I indicate that a text is *created by humans* to exclude natural objects and phenomena that have been literally or figuratively untouched by the human hand. In my view, a leaf is not a text, the sun is not a text, a microorganism is not a text, the wind is not a text. I add *indirectly* to include AI-generated texts, which are, in the ways I described in the previous section, made indirectly by humans.

By **pop culture text**, I mean any text that has been made available to a lot of people by today's circulation and distribution apparatuses (Storey, 2021). These apparatuses include social media and streaming services and more traditional apparatuses like film studios, record companies, and retailers. Pop culture texts might be created by the culture industries—say, a TV show—or by everyday people—say, a recap podcast about that TV show. If the text is accessible to a lot of people, it's a pop culture text. One final note: given the fragmentation of culture, I don't require a text to *actually be* accessed by a lot of people to count as a pop culture text. It doesn't actually have to be *popular*. It would simply have to be, via today's technological apparatuses, available to many people. As Storey notes, historically, definitions of pop culture have hinged on what pop culture is *not*: specifically, it is *not* high art or fine art. I don't find that distinction particularly useful today, but I do tend to make a distinction between a pop culture text and an academic text. I make this distinction because there tends to be a different set of attitudes and approaches to the texts young people engage with in and out of schools. My hope, particularly in the second half of the book, would be to draw young people's awareness to and question those distinctions.

In line with these definitions of *text* and *pop culture text*, I define **literacy** as the skills, practices, and habits of engaging with texts in order to construct meaning for use in any area of our lives. This understanding of literacy is connected to the sociocultural perspectives on literacy that have emerged over the past several decades (e.g., Lankshear & Knobel, 2006; Purcell-Gates et al., 2011; Street, 1994). I'll say more about the skills, practices, and habits involved in *engagement* below.

I define *meaning* in a—you guessed it—broad sense. One might engage with a text to understand a certain set of information. One might engage with a text to enter into a meaningful experience of connection or aesthetic pleasure. One might engage with a text to communicate with others, proximal or remote. There are endless ways of construing *meaning*, and my intention isn't to precisely delineate the contours of meaning a priori. I intend to emphasize that, when we read or write a text, we always get *something* out of it and that *something* has some sort of effect on our lives (Duke et al., 2006).

Pop Culture Literacy, then, simply includes the skills, practices, and habits required to construct meaning from pop culture texts. When it comes to pop culture, the distinction between the two major domains of print literacy, reading and writing, doesn't hold up as well. One might "read" a new pop song and then "write" a tweet about it, for example, but those activities are part of a larger practice of engagement. **Engagement**, in my view, is any sort of activity that is carried out in relation to texts. When it comes to how we support young people with their pop culture engagement, I've found it helpful to think of engagement in terms of three kinds of activities.

Interpretation: what we think. I define *interpretation* as what happens in our minds as we're consuming pop culture. What do we think about as we're watching a TV show or listening to a song? What do we notice and pay attention to in the text? Ultimately, interpretation is about what we think a text means and about what we draw on to construct that meaning. It can be difficult to disconnect interpretation from response and composition. After all, we can only perceive how another person is interpreting a text by listening to how they respond to it and watching what they do with it, and the act of discussing a text with others can shape and shift a person's initial interpretations. It's worth remembering that interpretation is ongoing and active, even when it's silent and invisible to others.

Response: what we say. *Response* refers to what we say about a text to others and includes both live, in-person discussions and social media interactions. We bring our interpretations to discussion, but the act of articulating those interpretations can shift, constrain, or broaden them. Digital responses include live tweeting a TV show, commenting on a YouTube video, or even sharing a link to a digital text. These forms of engagement move our otherwise private interpretations of texts into the daylight and create opportunities for engagement and discussion with others.

Composition: what we do. Finally, *composition* is a kind of doing. Memes, gifs, videos, images, songs, and dances are compositions. It's easy to see how rewriting a song's lyrics is an act of composition, but I argue that even the process of selecting a pre-existing text to post and circulate on social media counts as an act of composition. For example, selecting a meme to express something about oneself—a mood, a personality trait—is not a simple act of copying. It's a way of bringing an existing text into the larger "text" of one's social media persona.

Research

This inquiry began in a cramped, windowless guided reading room, after school every Friday, with a small group of young people: Audrey, Briana, Danielle, Jasmine, and Kaylee. I was researching how adolescent girls' engagements with pop culture shaped their understanding of themselves, as girls, and the world around them.

I carried out this research at Horizon Middle School, one school in a large regional network of charter schools for which I directed the literacy program. The study consisted of weekly meetings with this small group during which we'd engage with a pop culture text of their choosing together and then discuss our interpretations. In our first meeting, they selected the television shows *Modern Family*, *Empire*, *Black-ish*, and *Vampire*

Diaries; the *Step Up* movies; and songs by the artists A Boogie and Kodak Black.

At first, we interacted in a way that felt, to me, akin to teacher and students. I told them that they could call me *Mia* and that they could express themselves however they wanted to in our meetings, but it took a couple of weeks for them to do so. I found it hard to shake the teacher in me. In our first couple of meetings, I probably offered more of my own ideas than I should have, with too much frequency, clarity, and certainty. Over time, the group became more comfortable with its homegrown norms, and I learned to sit back (though I never fully overcame my proclivity to share when something in a text bothered or confused me).

Throughout this period, I continued to be a presence in the school—walking the hallways, meeting with their teachers during their off-periods, and observing their classes. Over time, they began to greet me more often when we saw each other, mentioning past meetings or asking about future meetings. I first noticed Briana referring to our meetings as "Group," asking, for example, "What are we doing for Group this week?" Wanting a simpler way of referring to our time together, I picked up on the name, and then it came to be more or less the official name of what was regarded as another elective after-school activity in the school community.

Audrey, Briana, Danielle, Jasmine, and Kaylee identified as heterosexual girls of color. Briana and Jasmine identify as Black Dominican, Danielle and Kaylee identify as Black, and Audrey identifies as Afro-Latina. I asked how they wanted to be referred to in this writing and offered a range of options (participants, young women, young people, students, and so on); they chose *girls*. The girls were connected to each other through friendship and their shared history at Horizon. While several pairs of them appeared to be long-standing close friends, with in-jokes and shared stories they'd call up and tell jointly, the group didn't seem to function as a cohesive group or clique. Audrey and Kaylee seemed to be closest at first, always sitting next to each other and building off each other's ideas. They both seemed to relish passing judgment on our shared texts—whether on the way women were made to appear or on the realism, or lack thereof, of situations and actions depicted.

Kaylee's voice and tone often sounded, to my ear, maternal, as she was likely to express both judgment and concern for girls and women putting themselves in precarious or embarrassing situations. Briana is funny, playful, and, while a dominant personality in the group, adept at playing off the rest of the girls, riffing on their comments and teasing them. Kaylee and Briana were the pair who most often brought up shared experiences to support their points (but, often as not, just to reminisce and story-tell). Danielle was the quietest of the group, and only in viewing the videos of our discussions did I realize that she often vied for airtime only to be drowned out by the rest of the girls. Danielle also shared history with the other girls—Kaylee, especially—but this shared history was seldom called upon in our discussions.

Our discussions lasted up to an hour, depending on the length of the text we viewed together. Our meetings ended naturally, when it felt like there was nothing left to say about the pop culture texts under discussion. The endings felt natural to me, but I typically made this judgment based on how far away from the topic their discussion had strayed. The girls took turns without my intervention, and they didn't seem to mind the frequent interruption and cross-talk. Occasionally, when it seemed like one was repeatedly cut off in her bid for a turn, I intervened to create an opening for her.

I observed that our discussions of pop culture texts both coalesced and fractured around the question *why*? Why do women on screen dress as they do? Why do they move and dance as they do? Who is in charge of shaping the way they appear? It is not surprising that this sort of explanatory mode of discussion would take hold. We were assembled in an academic setting, a classroom, and, whether or not I wanted to, I operated as a teacher-like figure. In such a setting, one that does not feel too dissimilar to their print-based English classes, explanations of texts are expected. So, in addition to their spontaneous, sometimes funny, sometimes raucous commentary, the girls developed coherent explanations of what they saw, supplying deliberate reasoning and evidence and drawing on academic language to do so.

In the first part of the book, each chapter includes a section called "Up Close." In this section, I reconstruct and narrativize these discussions to showcase what young people already do with pop culture texts—how they already interpret and respond to these texts and what meanings they make of them.

Chapters
Part One: Pop Culture Literacy Framework
Chapter 1: Active Engagement

This chapter presents the first part of the pop culture literacy framework: active engagement. I argue that young people are not passive recipients of messages and ideas found in pop culture but active participants in creating meaning. The chapter gives examples of how young people are already active in their engagement with pop culture and then suggests what teachers and schools can do to make young people's engagement even more active.

Chapter 2: Critical Engagement

This chapter presents the second part of the pop culture literacy framework: critical engagement. In this chapter, I provide background on the field of critical literacy and highlight four major points: texts are crafted objects, texts are not closed systems, critical readers are self-aware, and critical readers dwell in contradiction. From there, I give examples of how young people are already interpreting, responding to, and composing pop culture texts critically, and then show what teachers and schools can do to support young people in engaging with pop culture even more critically.

Chapter 3: Strategic Engagement

This chapter presents the third part of the pop culture literacy framework: strategic engagement. In this chapter, I suggest that young people must be just as strategic in their approach to pop culture texts as they are in their approach to academic texts. To be strategic, we must understand what is distinctive about how pop culture texts make meanings and messages available to their audiences. I describe two distinctive features of pop culture texts: multimodality and intertextuality. Then, I show how young people make sense of pop culture texts multimodally and intertextually. Finally, the chapter offers ideas of how teachers can help young people become more strategic readers of pop culture texts.

Part Two: Pop Culture Literacy Lessons

The lessons presented in Part Two can be taught as a unit of study or can be adapted to mesh with existing standards-aligned curriculum in English Language Arts, social studies, or advisory classes. Each chapter captures what is taught and learned in each part of the unit and provides multiple options for teaching the lessons in a variety of classroom settings.

Chapter 4: The Foundations of Pop Culture Literacy

This chapter offers five lessons that teach young people how to take up more intentional stances as readers of pop culture texts. These lessons invite young people to conduct an inquiry into their reading stances in relation to various academic and pop culture texts and hypothesize why they take particular stances in relation to particular texts. The lessons also invite them to practice interpreting, responding to, and composing pop culture texts in different ways, shifting their approach strategically depending on their purpose for reading.

Chapter 5: Layers of Story

This chapter's five lessons introduce the idea that there are hidden layers of story in texts. The lessons define and illustrate the layers of story across a wide variety of texts. In these lessons, students examine their own storytelling practices and learn three concepts that help them make connections between stories across texts: *storylines, character tropes,* and *probable stories.*

Chapter 6: Autoethnography

This chapter introduces students to the research genre of autoethnography: a form of personal storytelling that connects the personal to the cultural. The five lessons in this chapter take young people through the process of composing a multimodal autoethnography, highlighting the value of developing in young people a sense of intentionality and authorship in their own storytelling.

Three Caveats

Caveat One: The Water Wiggler Phenomenon. The problem with writing about pop culture is that, without specific examples, the concepts are limp on the page. Yet, with specific examples, the writing has dated itself before the ink dries. I use specific examples of pop culture texts and practices throughout the book, but this book is not *about* these specific examples. The examples are there to illustrate and enliven the concepts—concepts that, I hope, will outlast the particulars.

A sub-caveat to this caveat is that these examples come from *me*. I believe that, as educators, we must *walk the walk*, so to speak. That means, if we intend to help young people engage with pop culture more actively, critically, and strategically, we must push ourselves to do the same. By extension, in writing this book, I've tried to *walk the walk* with my own pop culture engagements, reflecting on the ways I have and haven't been active, critical, and strategic with pop culture. You'll get perhaps a deeper understanding of me as a pop culture consumer than you would've asked for.

Caveat Two: Who Are You Calling "We"? Throughout the book, I use "we" to refer to a collective of people who are consuming or engaging with pop culture. I use "we" not to be presumptuous—not to suggest that you and I engage with the same pop culture texts in the same ways. Maybe you love pop culture, or maybe you don't. Maybe you're, in today's internet parlance, *extremely online*, or maybe you're extremely not. I recognize that.

I use "we" because, in so many ways, the culture industries have positioned us as a *them*, as a mass of people (Adorno, 1991). To me, the response—the resistance—to that positioning is to take up that identity as a *we*. When it comes to my engagement with pop culture, I find it helpful and empowering to see myself as part of collectives and communities who are struggling and striving alongside each other and in similar ways. When I say "we," then, I don't mean everyone. I mean the audiences, the users, the viewers, the citizens, the real everyday people, young and old and in-between, who are engaging with pop culture.

Caveat Three: This Book Is Not About Mental Health. Much of the mainstream discourse about young people's engagement with pop culture—and social media, in particular—revolves around concerns about mental health (see especially Haidt, 2024). In the news, in conversations with friends and colleagues, and online, I hear that social media is addictive; that it causes anxiety, depression, and body dysmorphia; that it shortens attention spans; that it creates new avenues for bullying, and so on.

To what extent these claims are true is a question worthy of ongoing discussion, study, and scholarship. This question is, however, outside the purview of this book. This book is fundamentally about *literacy*, about helping young people develop active, critical, and strategic ways of engaging in the culture and, in doing so, making sense of themselves and the world around them.

Final Note: Concepts That Last

Over the coming years, as ever, young people will need to be just as creative in reinventing their ways of engaging with pop culture as the culture industries are in reinventing pop culture itself. In a month, year, or decade from now, not only will the examples of pop culture be different but the cultural milieu in which those examples are embedded will be different. In this book, my intention is to offer concepts that are broad enough to be durable: active engagement, critical engagement, strategic engagement. Only time will tell how young people—and you—will put those concepts into practice.

References

Adorno, T. (1991). *The culture industry: Selected essays on mass culture*. 2nd ed. Routledge.

Baudrillard, J. (1981/1994). *Simulacra and simulation* (S. F. Glaser, Trans.). University of Michigan Press.

Bezemer, J., & Kress, G. (2003). Changing text: A social semiotic analysis of textbooks. *Designs for Learning, 3*(1–2), 10–29.

Chayka, K. (2024). *Filterworld: How filters are changing how we see ourselves, and everything else*. Graywolf Press.

Duke, N. K., Purcell-Gates, V., Hall, L. A., & Tower, C. (2006). Authentic literacy activities for developing comprehension and writing. *The Reading Teacher, 60*(4), 344–355.

Federal Communications Commission. (1996). *1996 annual assessment of the status of competition in the market for the delivery of video programming*. www.fcc.gov/document/1996-annual-report

Forde, E. (2019, May 31). Oversharing: How Napster nearly killed the music industry. *The Guardian*. www.theguardian.com/music/2019/may/31/napster-twenty-years-music-revolution

Haidt, J. (2024). *The anxious generation: How advances in technology are hurting our children and what we can do about it*. Random House.

Hoel, E. (2024, March 29). AI-generated garbage is polluting our culture. *The New York Times*. www.nytimes.com/2024/03/29/opinion/ai-internet-x-youtube.html

Jameson, F. (1991). *Postmodernism, or the cultural logic of late capitalism*. Duke University Press.

Lankshear, C., & Knobel, M. (2006). *New literacies: Everyday practices and classroom learning*. Open University Press.

Lopez, J. (2002). *Jenny from the block* [Video]. www.youtube.com/watch?v=dly6p4Fu5TE

Lorenz, T. (2023). *Extremely online: The untold story of fame, influence, and power on the internet*. Simon & Schuster.

Martha and the Vandellas. (1964). Dancing in the street [Song]. On *Dance Party*. Gordy.

Purcell-Gates, V., Melzi, G., Najafi, B., & Orellana, M. F. (2011). Building literacy instruction from children's sociocultural worlds. *Child Development Perspectives, 5*(1), 22–27.

Reynolds, S. (2019, December 28). "Streaming has killed the mainstream": The decade that broke popular culture. *The Guardian.* www.theguardian.com/culture/2019/dec/28/overload-ambush-and-isolation-the-decade-that-warped-popular-culture-simon-reynolds

Storey, J. (2021). *Cultural theory and pop culture: An introduction.* 9th ed. Routledge.

Street, B. (1994). The new literacy studies: Implications for education and pedagogy. *Changing English, 1*(1), 113–126.

Tag Team. (1993). Whoomp! (There it is) [Song]. On *Whoomp! (There It Is).* Life Records.

Unwin, A., & Yandell, J. (2016*). Rethinking education: Whose knowledge is it anyway?* Bloomsbury Academic.

Wu, T. (2016). *The attention merchants: The epic scramble to get inside our heads.* Alfred A. Knopf.

Part One

Pop Culture Literacy Framework

1

Active Engagement

Just as my sixth-grade year was coming to a close, I found myself in a familiar situation: refusing to complete an assignment on principle. My classmates and I had been grouped up and assigned to write about ecosystems. My group got the rainforest. I'd decided, after the ritual sizing-up of my groupmates, and with an idea already in mind, that I'd take the lead on the project. Instead of writing a traditional paper, I suggested we rewrite a popular song's lyrics to be about the rainforest.

"Some song like, I don't know, 'Motownphilly,' or whatever," I probably said, straining to make the idea sound unconsidered.

The idea had been, of course, thoroughly considered. "Motownphilly" (Boyz II Men, 1991) was not only a favorite song of mine but also the musical backdrop of a memorable scene from *Full House* (Franklin et al., 1991) in which Stephanie Tanner dances triumphantly at the head of a V-formation. The episode was several seasons old at that point, but I must have just caught the rerun. I didn't have a simple rewrite of the lyrics in mind. Oh, no. I envisioned a full-on song-and-dance routine. I had been waiting for my life to supply an occasion to

DOI: 10.4324/9781032667027-3

write and choreograph this routine, and I just knew the rain-forest project was it.

Before my groupmates had a chance to voice what I can only imagine were deep reservations about my idea, the teacher floated over to us, and I pitched it. She gently suggested we could write the song as part of the presentation of our paper but that the song couldn't take the place of the paper itself.

Little did my teacher know, I had also been waiting for my life to supply an occasion to take a stand on the genre of a writing assignment. A few nights earlier, I'd watched an episode of *Blossom* in which Blossom Russo writes a paper in the form of a play, receives a B because she didn't do what was assigned, rejects the B, and then ratchets up the stakes by dropping out of the class, putting her upcoming graduation in jeopardy (D'Amore & Junger, 1995). I channeled Blossom's moxie—and, well, her obstinacy—as I made the case that we could demonstrate just as deep an understanding of the rainforest in song lyrics as we could in a paper.

Eventually, I lost that argument, as Blossom lost hers. But there may have been an appendix hastily paperclipped to our report the morning it was due, featuring the lyrics to the song "Rainforest Feelin'" (*Let's start with the can-o-py!/Doin' a little treetop thing . . .*).

Looking back, I can see that I was under the influence of quite a brew of pop culture references! There's the popular song I wanted to rewrite, the dance formation I wanted to replicate, the TV character's sense of triumph I wanted to claim for myself. And then there was the way another TV character emboldened me to create conflict—to create a plot—in my life where none had existed before.

I realize this anecdote isn't exactly universally relatable. Even if you know "Motownphilly" as well as I do and remember those episodes of *Full House* and *Blossom*, those references probably never came together in your mind to motivate an argument with your sixth-grade science teacher. My relationship to pop culture is particular. So is yours. And so are your students'. While pop culture gives us all ideas, what we do with those ideas is a brew entirely of our own making.

An Active Engagement Framework

Productive Consumption

In *Grundrisse*, Karl Marx (1939/1973) explained what he saw as the dialectical relationship between production and consumption, arguing that *consumption* always immediately entails *production*. He used biological processes to illustrate this point:

> . . . in nature the consumption of the elements and chemical substances is the production of the plant. It is clear that in taking in food, for example, which is a form of consumption, the human being produces his own body. But this is also true of every kind of consumption which in one way or another produces human beings in some particular aspect. (p. 24)

In other words, there is always something *produced* in the act of *consumption*. The commodities Marx had in mind when he wrote *Grundrisse*—in the mid-19th century—have little in common with the commodities I was working with when I composed "Rainforest Feelin'." So let's fast-forward to the 1980s when cultural theorists John Fiske and Stuart Hall applied Marx's notion of *productive consumption* to mass culture.

Encoding and Decoding

In "Encoding/decoding," Stuart Hall (1980) disputed the presumed inevitability that a consumer of a text will decode exactly the message the producer of the text intended. Hall used a televised newscast to illustrate the point. An event that occurs somewhere in the world doesn't become a *story* until a newscaster encodes it as such in a news broadcast and viewers then view that broadcast. In this set-up, the newscaster is the encoder, the broadcast is the message, and the viewer is the decoder. The newscaster does everything in their power to encode the message so that there's no discrepancy in how it will be decoded. Ideally, the viewer will notice exactly what the broadcaster wanted them to notice about the event and interpret its significance in exactly the way the broadcaster wanted them to interpret it. In Hall's framework, this kind of reading would be considered the preferred reading.

Hall (1980) argued that the preferred reading is only possible if and when both the encoder and the decoder operate according to the dominant cultural order and so bring the same set of assumptions and understandings to communicative codes. In most cases, then, the communication process isn't as airtight as the encoder might wish it to be. Some readings of a text are what Hall called *negotiated* or *oppositional*. In negotiated readings, the decoder accepts certain hegemonic definitions but "makes [their] own ground rules" (p. 60) about how those definitions play out on a specific level. I think of young girls playing with Barbies by changing them into outfits they consider prettier or more appealing to Ken. Appealing to a male gaze hasn't been challenged in this scenario, only Mattel's encoding of it. In oppositional readings, the decoder "detotalizes" the message the encoder intended "in order to retotalize it according to some alternative framework" (p. 61). I think of the young girl who plays with the Barbie by defacing and disfiguring it, disconnecting it from the beauty standards that condition its mass appeal (an oppositional reading that Mattel, ironically, re-appropriated as Kate McKinnon's character Weird Barbie in the 2023 blockbuster *Barbie* [Gerwig, 2023]).

Hall's taxonomy of readings highlights that pop culture consumers are not passive recipients of ideas, meanings, messages, or, as we would say today, *content*. As consumers of pop culture texts, we have some degree of choice when it comes to how we decode them.

Excorporation

Fiske (1989) went further, arguing that, as consumers, we actively rework a given commodity, "treating it not as a completed object to be accepted passively, but as a cultural resource to be used" (p. 8). According to Fiske, commodities can be used to "construct meanings of self, of social identity and social relations" (p. 9). To demonstrate this point, he offered the example of jeans. Jeans, to Fiske, are semantically abundant, their meanings multiple and dynamic. Once a workwear staple for industrial laborers and farmers, jeans became, by the time of Fiske's writing, a near-universal wardrobe staple for Americans. After an informal survey of his students (118 out of 125 of whom were wearing jeans on the day), Fiske concluded that these multiple meanings of jeans clustered around notions of Americanness. Jeans connoted values and qualities central to American mythology: freedom, toughness, hard work, leisure, and progress.

Fiske argued that wearing jeans didn't necessarily mean subordinating oneself to these values. He described how consumers could transform their jeans as a way of countering such values:

> If today's jeans are to express oppositional meanings, or even gesture toward such social resistance, they need to be disfigured in some way—tie dyed, irregularly bleached, or particularly, torn. If "whole" jeans connote shared meanings of contemporary America, then disfiguring them becomes a way of distancing oneself from those values. (p. 3)

Fiske referred to the process by which consumers make their own culture out of the commodities at hand as *excorporation*. He argued that, through this process, there is at least a partial transfer of power from the producer of the commodity to its consumer. Destroying one's jeans is "an assertion of one's right to make one's own culture out of the resources provided by the commodity system" (p. 12). (And yet, today, most jeans on the market come pre-distressed, whether by hand, sand, acid, or laser. As we see time and time again, the market is omnivorous, devouring the resistance to it and metabolizing it for profit.)

Pop Culture Consumption Today
Revisiting decades-old pop culture scholarship, I'm struck by how difficult it must have been to make the argument that both the meaning-making and social experiences of consuming pop culture were active. After all, the prevailing image of pop culture consumption in the 20th century was one of dead-eyed children, sitting motionless on a couch before the glowing square of the TV screen. Today, it's clear that pop culture consumers don't

simply sit themselves down in front of the TV (or laptop, tablet, or phone, as the case may be) and passively consume information and ideas. As we watch TV, play video games, or listen to music, we actively develop interpretations of these texts and, more and more, share and negotiate our interpretations through our social media feeds. What's more, when we share memes, participate in viral dance challenges, or post or comment on send-ups of pop songs on social media, we are actively consuming—and, in fact, *producing*—culture. Even the simple act of scrolling is active. It's a dance we do with algorithms, noting what they seem to think we want to see and seeking ways to coerce them into being right more often.

Social media has made our active engagement with pop culture more apparent than ever. Corporations may supply the raw material, but we're the ones who fashion it into something meaningful. Corporations can *suggest* meanings—as Mattel does, for example, when they supply a fully accessorized Barbie Fantasy Hair Doll with Mermaid and Unicorn Look™—but those meanings aren't simply copied into our minds. They're malleable enough to allow for adaptation, improvisation, and re-creation. And this type of consumption is not frivolous or merely play. We use the bits and pieces of culture that flow through our devices and our homes to construct both our public image and our personal mythology (Jenkins, 2006), to make sense of both our personal experiences and the world around us.

This is all to say that, if we're to support young people in understanding themselves and their worlds, we need to look through and beyond individual texts—songs, memes, music videos, TV shows, and so forth—to see what young people are actually doing with these texts and what meaning these activities hold for them. By redirecting our focus to active engagement, we might overcome our tendencies to obsessively overanalyze and critique the cultural products our students enjoy. (But maybe I should speak for myself. I'm a strongly self-identifying English major who never met a text she didn't want to overanalyze and critique!) When we're too focused on the texts, all we can do as educators is replace our students' interpretations with our own supposedly more enlightened interpretations. We miss the opportunity to help them develop strategies for reading, interpreting, and even critiquing and resisting the raw material the culture industries supply. And to do that, we need to start from an understanding of how people already actively engage with pop culture.

Snapshots: Active Engagement in Action

In this section, I present a series of examples of how everyday people actively engage with the pop culture texts supplied by the culture industries. I've sought examples that span time and demographics but that illustrate how active people can be in interpreting and responding to these texts—and even how creative they can be in composing their own pop culture texts.

The Birth of an Icon

In November 2019, Disney+, the on-demand streaming service, released *Star Wars: The Mandalorian*, the franchise's first live-action TV series (Favreau, 2019–present). It introduced the character The Child, popularly known as Baby Yoda, a member of Yoda's unnamed alien species. Fans of the show know Baby Yoda as Grogu. He was discovered when the Mandalorian and the droid IG-11 infiltrated an encampment on the planet Arvala-7.

I first knew Baby Yoda as a meme. In late 2019, my social media feeds were awash with Baby Yoda memes. Baby Yoda was "every mom on Christmas morning watching you open presents" (Benson, 2019). Baby Yoda was "you, watching your dad put batteries in your Gameboy after you put them in backwards six times" (TierneyColin, 2019). By November 2019, social media mentions of Baby Yoda outpaced mentions of the Democratic presidential candidates (Keegan, 2019). Baby Yoda also paid a visit to *Saturday Night Live*'s Weekend Update desk (King, 2019) and appeared on the cover of *The Hollywood Reporter*'s 2020 New Year's edition wearing a "Happy New Year!" sash under the cruelly ironic headline "A New Hope."

I saw, understood, and smiled at dozens of Baby Yoda memes in 2019, but I had to look up the part about the droid IG-11's infiltration of Arvala-7. That we can engage with a cultural product like Baby Yoda without knowing its provenance or back-story is one distinctive feature of today's pop culture landscape. So why is it that Baby Yoda memes became so popular? As James Poniewozik (2019) of the *New York Times* put it, *The Mandalorian* has "re-gifted us our childhoods," a characterization exemplified by the many versions of the meme that tap into familiar narratives of a heteronormative middle-class upbringing. While the image of Baby Yoda is novel, developed exclusively for this installment of the *Star Wars* franchise, it's also nostalgic, drawing on the franchise's rich iconography. Rebecca Keegan (2019), in the *Hollywood Reporter*'s cover story, argued that the rise of the memeable icon and the web culture that birthed it signals the decline of the traditional movie star and the studio systems that once cultivated stardom.

Baby Yoda will outlast the TV shows and films in which he appears, for we'll always be ready to graft new meanings and stories onto his adorably comforting visage. In this way, we are just as much the creators of Baby Yoda as George Lucas, *Star Wars*'s original auteur; Jon Favreau, *The Mandalorian*'s showrunner (2019–present); Christian Alzmann, the concept artist at Lucasfilm who's responsible for that adorably comforting visage; or Disney, the corporation behind the series.

Baby Yoda wasn't the first, isn't the most recent, and certainly won't be the last ferociously memeable icon. Among the very first was Grumpy Cat, an actual cat named Tardar Sauce who looked grumpy on account of her underbite and her feline dwarfism, according to her owners (McCarthy, 2013). The first image of Grumpy Cat was posted to Reddit in 2012. Unlike Baby Yoda, Grumpy Cat wasn't born an icon. Reddit users got right to work memeing Grumpy Cat, captioning photos of her with sardonic comments (for example, "There are two types of people in the world and I hate them both"). Grumpy Cat's career trajectory was steep and her ascendance swift. In 2013, she appeared in a YouTube series produced by Friskies cat food, and, in 2014, she appeared in Lifetime's *Grumpy Cat's Worst Christmas Ever* (Berlinger, 2014), in which she was voiced by famously deadpan actor Aubrey Plaza.

Each memeable icon comes with its own preset personality, whether determined by a nostalgic film franchise or by, well, a grumpy-looking face. But the internet can also do its own thing with an iconic character, distorting and stretching it beyond its intended meaning. Take the Duolingo owl, the language-learning app's cute cartoon mascot. Duolingo's notoriously aggressive push notifications inspired a Tumblr post of the owl holding a gun with the caption: "me: neglects my duolingo app" (knightcore, 2017). The post went viral, spawning many variations on the violent theme. In 2019, Duolingo tweeted an image of the owl standing in a doorway at night with the caption "coming soon," ostensibly to tease the upcoming release of its dark mode feature. This tweet reinvigorated the owl-as-murderer meme.

The Duolingo owl isn't the only icon that's been subjected to unwholesome memeification. AMC Theatre's *Dune: Part Two* promotional popcorn bucket met a similar fate in early 2024. The bucket was meant to resemble a sandworm, an extraterrestrial creature featured in the film. When images of the bucket were released, the internet quickly pointed out that the bucket looked more like a vagina. All of the memes—and *Saturday Night Live* sketches—you'd imagine followed in due course. The examples of Baby Yoda, Grumpy Cat, the Duolingo owl, and, yes, the *Dune* popcorn bucket illustrate that we, as pop culture audiences, don't sit by as culture washes over us. We remake and remix what the culture industries have to offer, finding in our active engagement nostalgia, connection, and humor.

Take, Replicate, Create

The music industry and its audiences have always enjoyed a dynamic symbiosis. Has anyone ever simply *listened to* pop music? We pipe it into our homes or directly into our ears, belt along to it in the car, dance to it, buy merch about it, and fancy it the soundtrack of the imagined movie of our lives. Record companies give us music, and then we *do something* with it. In recent years, TikTok has become something of an interloper in this sphere of activity, disrupting the mechanics of the industry–audience relationship in some cases but fine-tuning them in others. In this section, I examine how teens today actively engage in pop music and the unique role viral dance challenges play in that engagement.

Today's viral dances and dance challenges descend, but also depart, from the dance crazes of the past in several important ways. First, like the Twist of my parents' day or the Macarena (Los Del Rios, 1995) of mine, today's viral dances amplify and are amplified by the popularity of the songs to which they're choreographed. In some cases, everyday teens develop and popularize the dances, which, in turn, boosts the associated songs' popularity. In other cases, the artists or their choreographers create the dance, and teens simply follow the steps.

Second, record companies and artists have always relied on ancillary apparatuses to promote songs and to promote dances as a way of promoting songs. In the past, these apparatuses included TV shows like *American Bandstand* (1952–1989) in my parents' day or *Total Request* live (1998–2008) in mine. Today, however, the digital ecosystem of TikTok takes care of that for them.

Third, much of the actual dancing today takes place in bedrooms, backyards, and other domestic spaces, rather than in the communal spaces of clubs and concerts. But that doesn't mean there isn't a communality to a viral dance challenge. Individuals bond through virality, mutual recognition, and digital ritual rather than through skin, sweat, and body odor.

Finally, the entire life cycle of today's dances—inception, propagation, extinction—is often completely bound in digital space. A few bars of choreography can quickly go viral and then, just as quickly, disappear from memory, without anyone who isn't a chronically online teenager ever being the wiser.

My first brush with a viral dance was in early 2020 when I read about it in the *New York Times* (a classic elder Millennial scenario). The dance was called "Renegade." In early 2019, Atlanta rapper K Camp released the single "Lottery." Later that year, Jalaiah Harmon, then 14 years old, choreographed a dance to the song, posted a video of the dance on Funimate, and later cross-posted it on Instagram. Before long, the dance found its way to TikTok, where Charli D'Amelio, a teen dancer in her ascendance (she'd become TikTok's most followed user by spring of 2020 [Gluck,

2020]), posted her own version. The dance eventually went viral across multiple platforms. Until K Camp himself—and later the *New York Times*—recognized Harmon as the creator of the dance, its origins seemed diffuse and indiscernible. Diffuse, indiscernible origins, or the appearance of such, are another distinctive feature of today's pop culture landscape.

K Camp (2020) credited Harmon for making his song a hit. When the dance went viral, he renamed the song "Lottery (Renegade)" (2019) after the dance ("renegade" is repeated in the part of the song to which the dance is choreographed). The renaming was tactical, as the new name helped surface associated videos of the dance on TikTok and YouTube. It's striking that even something as seemingly fixed as a song's title is subject to change, should a new title help encourage circulation.

The "Renegade" dance exploded in popularity on the eve of the COVID-19 pandemic. The *New York Times* article I read was published on February 13, 2020 (Lorenz, 2020), and Harmon performed the dance at the NBA All-Star Game two days later on February 15. Just as "Renegade" was in its denouement, another viral dance was emerging. That same month, TikToker Keara Wilson, finding herself unimpressed by that day's TikTok dance challenges, decided to choreograph one of her own to rapper Megan Thee Stallion's single "Savage" (Pete et al., 2020). It only took five days for Megan Thee Stallion herself to post Wilson's dance, exponentiating its popularity (The Buzz, 2022). As the pandemic pushed us deeper into our devices, teens (and occasionally parents who were game) took up the "Savage" dance challenge with fervor. Thanks to the dance challenge, Megan Thee Stallion would become the most listened to artist on TikTok in 2020 with "Savage" being included in 30 million videos (Millman, 2020).

The dance to Megan Thee Stallion's more recent hit "Mamushi" (2024) followed a similar trajectory but with a few plot twists along the way. On June 20, 2024, Megan Thee Stallion released the single. On June 29, TikTok dancer MONA (@mona712_official) posted a dance she'd choreographed to the chorus (MONA, 2024). That same day, Megan Thee Stallion reposted MONA's video. On June 30, she posted a video of herself doing the dance—to great fanfare and appreciation in the comments section. The post all but ensured the dance's virality. On July 9, again to great fanfare and appreciation, Megan Thee Stallion posted a second video of herself performing the dance, this time in a Sailor Moon costume. (Sailor Moon is a popular manga character, and the song is a collaboration with Japanese rapper Yuki Chiba.) On July 30, Megan Thee Stallion once again reactivated the trend by posting a video of herself and a small group of backup dancers performing the dance in costume after a rally for then-presidential candidate Kamala Harris. The official music video was released on August 9, showcasing pieces of the viral dance's choreography.

We wouldn't call Keara Wilson or MONA *everyday* TikTok users. Whether or not by conventional standards, they're both professional dancers. But what's noteworthy is that they were not working on behalf of the artist or the record company. Their active engagement with the music ultimately amounted to marketing for the artist. So, on one hand, one could say that, as Fiske (1989) portended, these examples show how the power gap between the producer of a pop culture text and its consumer has shrunk. Social media has democratized so-called "content creation." Everyone is a producer, and everyone is a consumer. But, on the other hand, pop songs are still often produced, released, and marketed with corporate money. Dancers like Harmon and Wilson, don't see that money, nor do they see the kind of money white TikTokers like D'Amelio make by popularizing other people's, especially Black teens', dances. The difficulty in ascertaining what financial arrangements might exist between artists, their record companies, and TikTokers is part of the point. To wit: did Megan Thee Stallion have to pay @mona712_official for her choreography to use it in the official music video? It's unclear. (Wilson, for her part, copyrighted her choreography a year after the "Savage" dance went viral [Skinner, 2021].) TikTokers' participation in viral dances is at once creation, theft, and free labor. Consumption may be *productive*, as Marx (1939/1973) argued, but these examples show that consumption doesn't necessarily produce something new. In this case, it reproduces the existing inequities of the market.

Still, sometimes active engagement with pop music can feel downright wholesome. In 2024, synth-pop singer-songwriter Chappell Roan began to surge in popularity, even though she had been releasing critically acclaimed music since 2015. Her single "Hot to Go" (Amstutz & Nigro, 2023), soared in popularity boosted by not a viral dance per se, but a viral dance "tutorial" (scare quotes intended).

In the song's music video (Zhou, 2023) and in concerts, Roan opens the number by teaching the dance's ruthlessly simple moves (think: YMCA [Morali & Willis, 1978] but with the letters *H, O, T, T, O, G, O*). Fans' own versions of the tutorial went viral in the first half of 2024. TikTokers posted videos of themselves teaching, or pretending to teach, the dance to their friends ("True allyship is letting your queer friends teach you the hot to go dance" [Niki, 2024]); to the pope (@brittymigs playing the pope's "PR lady" [Migs 2024]); to pets ("Teaching my cat the hot to go dance because her mom is a lesbian so no way is she not learning it [Maya, 2024]); to livestock ("teaching the steers the hot to go dance by chappel roan because who else is going to" [McGrath, 2024] and "teaching the sheep the hot to go dance because no one else will" [Lorelei, 2024]); to ghosts (@essysparrow taught it to "all the ghosts in this ancient valley" [Sparrowgirl, 2024] and @abbysworldsastage to Tolkien at his gravesite [Abbysworldsastage, 2024]); and, finally, to inanimate objects (@hannahjane.w taught it to "the teddy I've had from birth" [Hannah, 2024]).

To make sense of this virality, we must tap into the spirit of Roan's original tutorial. The music video, released the same day as the song in August 2023, opens with Roan teaching her grandparents the dance in (presumably) their home in Springfield, Missouri. The video is suffused with Americana and heartland imagery: monster trucks, construction sites, old-timey gas stations, livestock. Roan is in cheerleading drag, which underlines the dance's cheerleading origins. The video also features two local drag queens dancing and posing alongside her. The video's humor and narrative tension is held in the contrast between the queer-coded, campy mise-en-scene, costuming, and lyrics and the small-town Midwestern setting.

I take the video to be joyfully depicting a kind of queer evangelism. Roan is bringing not just her queer identity but the artifacts of queer culture to her hometown. She's teaching her grandparents the dance, spreading the word about the delights of queerness in a space traditionally read as unwelcoming to it. What I see, then, in the viral dance tutorial is an extension of the evangelical spirit of the original video. The in-group bonding of participating in the tutorial—whether at her concerts or on TikTok—is not exclusionary or insular. To the contrary, in teaching the dance, Roan's fans gesture toward bringing others in, be it their friends, their pets, or the pope. A motif of their captions, in fact, suggests this: they are teaching the dance *because who else is going to?*

These examples of viral dances, whether they feature top-down or bottom-up creative activity, illustrate how the music industry assumes that audiences will engage actively, and creatively, with its products. They don't just *allow* for this engagement. They encourage and even depend on it. This assumption rounds out my list of the distinctive features of today's pop culture landscape—a landscape inhabited by all of us but perhaps ruled by the young people we teach.

Active Engagement in the Classroom

Active Engagement Up Close
Platforms like TikTok, Facebook, and YouTube let us put our active engagement on display. What might active engagement with pop culture look and sound like in everyday classroom conversation, and how can we teach in a way that supports and enhances it? Let's listen in on Audrey, Briana, Danielle, and Kaylee's early pop culture discussions and take a closer look at two forms of their engagement: *character affiliation* and *probable stories*.

Character Affiliation
It was pajama day at Horizon Middle when we gathered in Ms. Corrigan's room to discuss the pilot of the girls' favorite show

Empire. The room was stuffy, as usual, and the pajamas weren't helping. Briana appointed herself to fetch a fan from a nearby classroom, though the time she took to do this suggested she was in pursuit of more interesting conversation elsewhere.

Audrey, Danielle, Kaylee, and I decided to begin without her. These were still early days, and our conversation, much like our tiny intervention room lined with boxes of guided reading books, felt a bit constrained. As we began talking, we felt the absence of Briana's irreverent energy.

"So what do we think about the way Cookie dresses?" I asked, as I turned back to my laptop and fiddled with the progress bar, looking for a good shot of Cookie's outfit in the climactic scene. The week before, our conversation had blossomed at the mention of Gloria's costuming on *Modern Family*, so I was hoping this question would coax some interest out of the group. To my eye, Cookie and Gloria dress similarly: tight knit dresses that reveal cleavage, high heels, bright colors, and dramatic prints.

"She's pretty," Kaylee replied, as she twirled a pencil stub she'd found inside the desk.

"Very pretty," Audrey echoed. She seemed to sense my desire for something more, so, after a pause, she sat up, took a breath, and began to elaborate. "She goes above and beyond. Like, everyone else is just wearing regular clothes, and she's taking her past personality into her clothing."

Longing for direct references to the text, as an English teacher does, I suggested we take a look at her appearance. I finally found the scene I had been looking for, when Cookie tries to take over a board meeting at Empire Records. In the pilot, Cookie is trying to regain control of the company she started with her ex-husband Lucious. She has just been released from prison after serving a 17-year sentence for dealing drugs, arguably having taken the fall for Lucious to protect their company. Dressed in a short animal-print dress, fur coat, and oversized sunglasses, she barges into the boardroom and announces her intention to take back Empire. The members of the board, dressed conservatively in dark suits, watch in stillness as Lucious ushers her out of the room and his son Andre takes over the meeting. I paused the scene as Cookie strides down the length of the boardroom.

"She makes sure she stands out and looks unique," Danielle said.

"And she tries to make sure that she's the one that is being seen, not the other people," Audrey added. "She wants everyone to watch her."

As if on cue, Briana appeared in the doorway with the fan. She plugged it in and turned it on with elaborate effort, only to turn it off again a few moments later so we could hear soft-spoken Danielle's uncharacteristically lengthy analysis.

"When she came back from jail, she wanted to have the power she had before she went to jail. She believes that nothing has changed, but a lot has changed. The way she dresses really shows who she is as a person because she's very sassy and messy and the type of clothes she wears—you're like, she's *something*. She's a pretty powerful woman, she speaks her mind, she tells people what it is right then and there."

As Danielle spoke, Briana's mind seemed to be in overdrive piecing together what she'd missed and formulating what would be, for the time being, the final word on the topic: "Yeah, the type of stuff a person likes, or the type of clothes they wear, it shows who they are as a person, what they're like as a person."

There is much to pay attention to in TV shows: story elements such as plot and character development and multimodal elements such as set design, costuming, and music. In these early conversations, I wanted to know what the girls paid attention to as they watched. After all, what we pay attention to shapes how we interpret and respond to a text.

It quickly became clear that the answer to this question, and several others I didn't even know to ask, was *Cookie*. Danielle, Audrey, Kaylee, and Briana did more than pay attention to Cookie; they *affiliated* with her. They identified with her desires and motivations and focused their responses to the text on her inner world.

I first started picking up on the girls' affiliation with Cookie when they discussed her style of dress. The girls had ridiculed Gloria's costuming, chalking up her gratuitous sexiness to straight male producers catering to a straight male audience. But in the discussion of Cookie, they did something very different.

They drew on their understanding of the show's narrative elements to make sense of her appearance. They didn't criticize her style of dress at all. Instead, they connected her clothes to her inner world, explaining how her clothes reflect her personality and advance her goals.

Because they affiliated with Cookie, they took care to explain why *she* would choose to dress in a particular way, rather than why *costumers* or *producers* would dress her in that way. They analyzed how Cookie dressed just as they'd analyze how someone they know in real life dresses. This is one tell-tale sign that we're affiliating with a character: we talk about them as if they're a real person.

Viewers who affiliate with a character often also find themselves defending and rationalizing the character's actions. Later in our discussion of *Empire*, the girls discussed how male and female characters are shown to manage their feelings differently.

> **Kaylee**: They take it out in different ways. Lucious takes it out in aggression and anger, and Cookie tries to, like, not be that aggressive.
>
> **Mia**: But hold on. Didn't she beat her son with a broom?
>
> **Audrey**: Well, that's her son! That's her son, and he's talking to her like she's any type of person—
>
> **Kaylee**: He called her a b-word!
>
> **Audrey**: Like if that was my mother?
>
> **Danielle**: That's any mother because if someone raised you, and they gave birth to you—
>
> **Audrey**: She wouldn't even have taken the time to, like, talk it out.
>
> **Mia**: So, based on this show, women can also have aggression then.
>
> **Danielle**: Yes, yes, they can. If they're provoked. In certain situations, yes.

At my mention of the broom incident, the girls erupted in passionate defense of Cookie, and, just as they did when we discussed how Cookie dresses, they animated her feelings, desires, and even rationalizations.

The literacy scholar Frank Serafini (2015) describes the process of reading a multimodal text as making an "interpretive path" through the text. Because there is so much to notice in a multimodal text, each reader makes their own path. Some readers tend to follow visual elements, and others tend to follow verbal elements. Some paths are shaped more by a desire to know what the creators of the text intended, others are shaped by background knowledge or personal experience, and still others are shaped by the social setting in which the text is read.

Character affiliation can shape a viewer's interpretive path through a TV show, as it did for the girls. Their attention, curiosity, and enthusiasm followed Cookie. While it may be to the show's advantage to inspire its viewers to affiliate with a character, the producers couldn't have predicted or prescribed this response for all of their viewers. Presumably, some viewers and fans of the show affiliate with Cookie, and others don't. This sort of consumption is active because it is what the girls chose to do with the text before them.

I came to see that, through their affiliation with her, the girls vicariously experienced the strength, power, and righteousness they admired. Cookie was invoked often over the course of our time together as an aspirational figure, an antidote to other representations of girls and women on screen. There's undeniable power for young people in that sort of affiliation, even if it does make them less critical of the text itself.

Character Affiliation: Key Points

When a viewer affiliates with a character,

- ◆ that character shapes the viewer's path through the text. They pay special attention to elements of the text that relate to that character
- ◆ the viewer seeks to understand the character's inner world—their feelings, traits, and motivations—and defend or rationalize their actions

◆ the viewer tends to talk about the character as if they are a real person, rather than analyzing the character as part of a text

◆ the viewer can experience feelings and situations vicariously through the character

Probable Stories

A week earlier, in our first official group meeting, we watched and discussed *Modern Family*, a show only Jasmine seemed to genuinely like. The rest of the group had assented half-heartedly to her recommendation, and a lot of the discussion was taken up reviewing the show's basic premises. *Wait, why did she marry that old guy? Who is the blonde girl married to? Is the blonde girl related to the old guy? Did Sofia Vergara have the kid with the old guy or some other guy?* Without a character to affiliate with—without a Cookie—the girls stayed in this sort of explanatory mode throughout most of the discussion.

Once we worked out the mechanics of the episode's plot, I asked the girls if they thought the depictions of women on the show were positive, negative, or both.

"Both," several girls murmured, perhaps buying some time to complete their mental calculations.

After a few more seconds of thought, Jasmine said, "The women in the show, their only interest—like when Gloria was doing her nails—they only care about how they look."

"Do we think that's true of all the women on the show?"

"It looks like it takes a long time for all of them to get dressed in the morning," Kaylee responded.

The girls went on, comparing and contrasting the characters' outfits and explaining how the women's interest in their appearance was used to move the episode's plot along (for example, the characters Haley and Alex claimed to have been out shopping when their parents tried to reach them, when, in fact, they had never returned from their vacation in New York). Meanwhile, Briana, unusually quiet, drummed her fingers on the desk. She seemed to still be at work calculating whether the portrayal of women was positive or negative, as the other girls layered in new variables, complicating the mathematics.

"But they don't pick it!" she finally interjected, perhaps figuring out something important as she spoke. "They make Claire wear something that—just because she doesn't have a lot of curves, she wasn't blessed—so they don't make her wear the stuff that Gloria's wearing. They don't get to wear their own clothes. The producer picks it for her. And that's something that kind of bothers me."

"But I think it's kind of positive 'cause, like, you obviously want to look good when you go outside. You don't want to look weird," Kaylee responded.

"But she doesn't get to pick what she wants, so that can really bother someone when they're working, and they make you wear something that's inappropriate."

Kaylee shrugged, and Audrey stepped in on Kaylee's behalf. "To connect it to how kids feel, you probably see a girl caring more about what they're wearing than a boy. A boy would probably, like, throw on whatever he wants, and a girl, she probably takes a very long time getting dressed."

To settle the argument in Kaylee's favor, Audrey told what I call a *probable story*. A probable story is a hypothetical scenario invented in the moment of discussion to fill gaps in an interpretation of another story. They serve to explain, elaborate, or support arguments about the text under discussion. To use Hall's (1980) terms, a probable story is an act of simultaneous *decoding* and *encoding*.

In this case, Kaylee and Briana were arguing about why the women on screen appear as they do. Kaylee acknowledged that the characters were very done-up, but, ultimately, she posited that the way they appear simply reflects the common desire to not look "weird" out in the world. Briana argued that Gloria's costuming reflects the producers' desire to show off her curves, and she rejected the idea that anyone—let alone Sofia Vergara, the actor who plays Gloria—would choose to dress that way. Audrey told a probable story as a way of arguing that, yes, women *do* choose to dress that way and, more to her point, to put effort into their appearance.

As it happened, Audrey's probable story settled the argument, but only temporarily. The conversation drifted off into explanations of why Gloria, who looks like *this*, married Jay, who looks like *that*, and Kaylee and I recalled a cringeworthy joke about the mismatch from the episode. When we eventually returned to the topic of why Gloria is dressed as she is, the group was more sympathetic to Briana's point that producers always want to show women's bodies to cater to their audience—a point that would be lost a week later when we discussed why Cookie was dressed similarly.

Over our time together, Audrey proved to be a master probable storyteller, conjuring stories to explain elements of texts and, as we see in this case, attempt to settle disagreements. Her probable story in this case exemplifies some of the key features of the genre (see the inset below).

Analysis of Audrey's Probable Story

"To connect it to how kids feel (4), you probably (1) see a girl (2) caring more about what they're wearing than a boy. A boy (2) would probably (1), like, throw on whatever he wants (3), and a girl, she probably (1) takes a very long time getting dressed (3)."

1. The patterns of language within the story suggest that these scenarios are seen as common occurrences. Audrey uses *probably* three times, but I also heard *most likely, usually*, and *nowadays* in other examples.
2. In her telling, Audrey smooths over all texture and specificity, which further indicates that she sees the scenario as universal.
3. Identity positions—in this case, gender—are central to the supposed logic of the story: *boys do this, girls do that.*
4. The probable story carries a sense of certainty and authority. It conveys a supposed universal truth about "how kids feel."

One of the dangers of the probable story is how effective it is at reinforcing stereotypes through circular logic. In Audrey's example, the girl taking "a very long time getting dressed" is offered up as an example that supports the idea that girls care more about their appearance than boys do. But, of course, the girl in question is made-up—a result of the stereotype rather than an example of it.

Probable stories are a form of active engagement because, like character affiliation, they cannot be predicted or prescribed by the creators of the text that elicited them. They are actively improvised by readers. They are a method not only of interpretation but also of response, as we see when they're used to convince others of the storyteller's thinking. The example of probable stories reminds us again that not all active engagement is critical. In Audrey's example and others like it, a reader actively invents a story, but that story cites age-old stereotypes and frames them as common sense.

Probable Stories: Key Points

Probable stories

- ◆ are improvised in discussion to fill gaps in the interpretation of another story
- ◆ frame hypothetical scenarios as common or even universal experiences
- ◆ rely on identity positions—and often stereotypical ideas about those identity positions—to make sense
- ◆ carry a sense of certainty and authority

Teaching Possibilities

If young people are already actively engaging with pop culture, what role might we as educators play in enhancing their pop culture literacy practices? Our first answer might be a hope that the young people in our care become even more active in their engagement. We'd want to guide them toward new ways of engaging with the TV shows, movies, social media platforms, and songs they love, and we can create opportunities for them to do so in our classrooms.

But the kind of pop culture pedagogy I envision requires, first and above all, *awareness*. Before we can teach young people new ways of actively engaging in pop culture, we need them first to become aware of themselves as readers and writers of pop culture texts, recognizing when and why they're drawn to certain texts, how they make sense of them, how they interpret and apply their meanings to their own lives, how they talk about them, and what they can and do create as part of that engagement. If we skip this step, our use of pop culture in the classroom will amount to an assortment of fun activities that do little more than momentarily capture young people's attention. So, in addition to creating opportunities for young people to engage in new ways, we want to create occasions for them to reflect on what they're already doing and what meaning their actions hold for them.

Table 1.1 lays out what this work might entail. These ideas reflect new ways of thinking about engagement with both academic and pop culture texts. Chapters 4–6 offer lessons built on the foundation of active engagement, but the ideas here can be incorporated into the daily rhythms of any English, humanities, or advisory class.

TABLE 1.1 Supporting active interpretation, response, and composition in the classroom.

Interpretation

Invite students to reflect on the kinds of pop culture texts they like and why, what they think about as they're engaging with those texts, and what they think about after engaging with those texts (in other words, what sticks with them).

Invite students to compare and contrast their experiences engaging with academic and pop culture texts:

◆ Which kind of experience is more active, and which is more passive? Why might that be?
◆ Do you do the same or different kinds of thinking when you engage with academic and pop culture texts?

(Continued)

TABLE 1.1 (Continued)

Interpretation

- ◆ Do you reach the same or different kinds of conclusions about what academic and pop culture texts mean?
- ◆ Are the messages and meanings of academic and pop culture texts you read similar or different?

Response

Invite students to reflect on whether and under what conditions they engage with others in online or in-person discussions of academic and pop culture texts.

Create opportunities for students to respond to pop culture texts in discussion as a way of negotiating the meanings and messages of these texts.

Create opportunities for students to discuss academic texts in online spaces as we often do when we discuss pop culture texts. Students can use online discussion boards, secure social media channels, or blog posts and comments to discuss academic texts.

Composition

Invite students to reflect on whether and under what conditions they compose their own texts when they engage in pop culture (e.g., Do they participate in viral dance challenges? Do they create memes? Do they use social media to post creative hot takes on pop culture?).

Create opportunities for students to compose their own multimodal texts—memes, gifs, videos, images, songs, and so forth—as a way of engaging with academic and pop culture texts. These compositions can be used as a way of either developing or demonstrating understanding of those texts.

Exercises for Teachers

Strong curriculum originates in a multidimensional understanding of our students' existing strengths and practices. A multidimensional understanding requires that we first hold our attention on the knowledge and capacities students bring to our classrooms. But we won't be able to fully appreciate and understand what we observe without firsthand experience with their practices. To that end, Chapters 1–3 offer a set of interpretation, response, and composition exercises for teachers or groups of teachers to complete on an ongoing basis, as they're moved to do so.

Interpretation Exercises

Reflect on the following:

- ◆ What was the last pop culture text that captivated you while you were engaged with it?

- What are some of the texts that have stuck with you after you were engaged with them? Are those the same texts as those that captivated you in the moment?
- What happens in your mind when you're engaging with those texts in the moment and when you're thinking back on them? Does your mind do something similar or different?
- What has the text done to your own thinking about yourself, your life, and what you see in the world?

Response Exercises

Choose a pop culture text that has been on your mind and respond to it either online or in in-person discussion with someone. Whether online or in person, track the mode of "talk" over the course of the discussion. Are you and others explaining, describing, storytelling, criticizing, analyzing, evaluating?

Is there any evidence of character affiliation coming out in the discussion? Does anyone tell a probable story as part of their response?

Composition Exercises

Use pop culture tools to compose a text that captures something meaningful, interesting, or funny about your life. Share with others (privately or on social media—it's up to you!). For example:

- Select and share an existing meme or gif
- Compose your own meme or gif
- Compose a longer multimodal text (song parody, dance challenge, video)

Final Note: Resisting the Temptations to Romanticize and to Criticize

As educators, we may sometimes fear the harmful influence of pop culture. It's true that pop culture is more pervasive than ever, more enmeshed in young people's lives than ever, and that its ability to stereotype, distort, erase, or misrepresent individuals and communities is as powerful as ever. But it's also true that everyday people, including the young people we teach, have more tools than ever to reinterpret and reinvent it, even to critique and resist it. Our students are not those mesmerized children sitting in front of the TV. In the midst of a global pandemic, they created dance crazes, invented TikTok challenges, and remixed old memes and gifs to speak to the trials of that extraordinary time. This is to say that what young people are doing on their phones all day doesn't need to feel as mysterious or worrisome as it often does.

I've offered active engagement as a framework that can help us direct our attention away from the pop culture texts themselves—including texts that we may find, in one way or another, objectionable—and toward young people's engagements with them. The active engagement framework has helped me resist the temptation to be overly critical of the texts that are circulating, and recognize how these texts—even those I may find objectionable—can be resources for self-expression and creativity.

I want to end, however, on a cautionary note. While engagement is, indeed, active and fascinatingly complex, and while it can be a site of resistance and critique, it still can and regularly does reinforce all sorts of limited ideas about people and communities. Active engagement can and regularly does trade in stereotypes, in binary notions of gender that erase a range of lived experiences, and in consumerist attitudes that reduce our identities to the things we buy. And, simply put, most active engagement in pop culture ultimately serves to enrich the rich. In this work, then, I strive to resist two opposing temptations: the temptation to criticize what young people do with pop culture texts and the temptation to romanticize it.

References

Abbysworldsastage [@abbsworldsastage]. (2024, May 28). Before anyone says it's disrespectful, I really admire Tolkien. We actually brought flowers . . . [Video]. TikTok.

Amstutz, K., & Nigro, D. (2023). Hot to go [Song; recorded by Chappell Roan]. On *The Rise and Fall of a Midwest Princess*. Island; Amusement.

Benson, J. [@TheJulieBenson]. (2019, November 29). *Every mom on Christmas morning watching you open presents* [Post]. X. https://x.com/TheJulieBenson/status/1200522618597605376

Berlinger, J. (Director). (2014). *Grumpy Cat's worst Christmas ever* [Film]. Lifetime.

Boyz II Men. (1991). Motownphilly [song]. Motown.

The Buzz. (2022). *Keara Wilson talks creating "The Savage Challenge" and capitalizing on her notoriety* [Video]. YouTube. www.youtube.com/watch?v=H3oYOTBXdi0

D'Amore, D. (Writer) & Junger, G. (Director). (1995, March 20). You say tomato (Season 5, Episode 20) [TV series episode]. In D. Reo, P. J. Witt, T. Thomas, G. Reynolds, D. Amico, J. D. Allison, & A. Katz (Executive Producers), *Blossom*. ABC Studios.

Duolingo [@duolingo]. (2019, March 26). *Coming soon* [Post]. X. https://x.com/duolingo/status/1110560261600149509

Favreau, J. (Executive Producer). (2019–present). *The Mandalorian* [TV series]. Lucasfilm; Golem Creations.

Fiske, J. (1989). *Understanding popular culture*. Unwin Hyman Ltd.

Franklin, J., Hur, S., Schimmel, J. (Writers) & Zwick, J. (Director). (1991, November 5). Gotta dance (Season 5, Episode 1) [TV Series Episode]. In J. Franklin, T. L. Miller, R. L. Boyett, D. Rinsler, & M. Warren (Executive Producers), *Full house*. Lorimar Studios, Stage 28.

Gerwig, G. (Director). (2023). *Barbie* [Film]. Warner Bros. Pictures.

Gluck, R. (2020, December 1). Charli D'Amelio makes history with TikTok records. *Guinness World Records*. www.guinnessworldrecords.com/news/2020/12/charli-damelio-makes-history-with-tiktok-records-640513

Hall, S. (1980). Encoding/decoding. In S. Hall, D. Hobson, A. Lowe, & P. Willis (Eds.), *Culture, Media, Language* (pp. 128–138). Routledge.

Hannah [@hannahjane.w]. (2024, May 30). This is snowy, please compliment his belly button, thanks [Video]. TikTok.

Jenkins, H. (2006). *Convergence culture: Where old and new media collide*. New York University Press.

K Camp. (2019). Lottery (renegade) [Song]. On *Wayy 2 Kritical*. Rare Sound; Empire; Interscope.

K Camp. [@kcamp]. (2020, February 14). Thank you Jalaiah and Skylar for helping make lottery the BIGGEST song in the world. Tell the blogs eat it up! [Post]. X. https://x.com/kcamp/status/1228506154650734593

Keegan, R. (2019, December 19). In Baby Yoda, Hollywood sees its past, present and meme-able future. *The Hollywood Reporter.* www.hollywoodreporter.com/movies/movie-features/baby-yoda-represents-past-present-future-hollywood-1263588/

King, R. [Director]. (2019, December 14). Scarlet Johannson/Neill Horan (Season 45, Episode 9). *Saturday Night Live.* SNL Studios.

knightcore. (2017, October 24). *me: *neglects my duo lingo app** [Post]. Tumblr. https://knightcore.tumblr.com/post/166742461758/me-neglects-my-duo-lingo-app-the-duolingo-owl

Lorelei [@folklorx]. (2024, April 29). All this work to teach them and still can't get tickets for the show in Richmond [Video]. TikTok.

Lorenz, T. (2020, February 13). The original Renegade. *The New York Times.* www.nytimes.com/2020/02/13/style/the-original-renegade.html

Los Del Rios. (1995) Macarena [Song]. On *A Mí Me Gusta.* RCA.

Marx, K. (1939/1973). *Grundrisse.* Penguin Books.

Maya [@evermoremaya]. (2024, April 29). daisy is a real one for this [Video]. TikTok.

McCarthy, E. (2013, October 16). 16 fun facts about Grumpy Cat. *Mental Floss.* http://mentalfloss.com/article/53217/16-fun-facts-about-grumpy-cat

McGrath, T. [@tylerthefarmer]. (2024, April 19). Another hard days work being a farmer [Video]. TikTok

Migs, B. [@brittymigs]. (2024, July 2). Part 7 P-O-P-E pope and pope [Video]. TikTok

Millman, E. (2020, December 16). Megan Thee Stallion is TikTok's most listened-to artist in 2020. *Rolling Stone.* www.rollingstone.com/pro/news/tiktok-megan-thee-stallion-year-end-2020-1104458/

MONA. [@mona712_official]. (2024, June 29). 流れる星達どこに向かう #yukichiba [Video]. TikTok.

Morali, J., & Willis, V. (1978). YMCA [Song; recorded by Village People]. On *Cruisin'.* Casablanca Records.

Niki [@nikimcc]. (2024, April 1). She's ready for Chappellchella [Video]. TikTok.

Pete, M., White, A., & Session Jr., B. (2020). Savage [Song; recorded by Megan Thee Stallion]. On *Suga*. 300 Entertainment.

Poniewozik, J. (2019, December 12). Baby Yoda is your god now. *The New York Times*. www.nytimes.com/2019/12/12/arts/television/baby-yoda-mandalorian.html

Serafini, F. (2015). Paths to Interpretation: Developing students' interpretive repertoires. *Language and Literacy, 15*(3), 118–133.

Skinner, P. (2021, August 2). The TikToker who created the viral "Savage" dance is copyrighting the moves. *BuzzFeed News*. www.buzzfeednews.com/article/paigeskinner/savage-dance-copyrighted

Sparrowgirl [@essysparrow]. (2024, July 12). hiked 8km to do this, i think they liked it [Video]. TikTok.

TierneyColin. (2019). *The "baby Yoda" memes may be getting annoying, but thought everyone would get a kick out of this one* [Post]. Reddit. www.reddit.com/r/retrogaming/comments/dzmi54/the_baby_yoda_memes_may_be_getting_annoying_but/

Wilson, K. [@keke.janajah]. (2020, March 10). Part 9 NEW DANCE ALERT! [Video]. TikTok. www.tiktok.com/@keke.janajah/video/6802722722389576965?lang=en

Zhou, J. (2023). *Hot to go* [Video]. YouTube. www.youtube.com/watch?v=xaPNR-_Cfn0

2

Critical Engagement

In late 2021, *And Just Like That* (King, 2021–present), the self-styled "new chapter" of *Sex and the City* (Star, 1998–2004), premiered on HBO Max. The reboot caused commotion among my cohort of elder Millennial New York women. The original series ran through our high school and college years. I didn't watch it until the year after college, my first year as a teacher, when a sanitized version—highly so, I'd later find out—ran in syndication on TBS. For me and many of my friends, watching *Sex and the City* (and rewatching and rewatching it) was a core coming-of-age experience.

Since *Sex and the City*'s premiere, audiences have felt called to identify with one of the four main characters. The fervor, of course, has sustained a cottage industry of merchandise emblazoned with slogans like "I'm a Carrie!" or "I can't keep calm. I'm a Miranda." Chelsea Fairless and Lauren Garroni, the duo behind the Instagram account and podcast *Every Outfit* (2021–present), have made being a Miranda a badge of honor. In late 2019, some 15 years after the series finale aired on HBO, Fairless and Garroni published a book called *We Should All Be Mirandas: Life Lessons from* Sex and the City's *Most Underrated Character*.

Sex and the City pulled a generation of women into a dialogue about what it meant to be a woman. As Megan Garber (2019)

DOI: 10.4324/9781032667027-4

described this sort of dialogue: men invent the categories, and women are expected to slot themselves into them. Yes, you could reject the premise of this culturally coerced character affiliation, but even rejecting a premise is a way of engaging with a premise.

In my world, *And Just Like That*'s premiere was a big moment, and, fighting my own late-pandemic ennui, I decided to meet that moment by meticulously documenting my reactions to each episode on Instagram Stories for a small group of friends whom I knew would be watching along. The Stories were part-recap, part-reaction video, and part-literary analysis. I was thrilled to opine, to make cheap jokes, to point out continuity errors, to search for meaning in a show that, it became increasingly clear, offered little more than breadcrumbs of meaning.

In one of the richer exchanges, my friend Stephanie and I discussed the show's clumsy efforts to diversify the cast by having each of the three main characters make a new friend of color. In the episode "Some of My Best Friends" (Robespierre, 2021), Miranda bonds with her new friend Nya over dinner, a scenario that strained credulity after Miranda's bungled attempts to demonstrate anti-racism in her early interactions with Nya came out as racial microaggressions. Stephanie feared that their attempts at establishing these friendships would come off as "if Black women/WoC [women of color] just understood where white women were coming from . . " Miranda's faux pas were played for laughs; there was no closer examination of her instinct to center her supposed anti-racism in her interactions with people of color. To Stephanie's point, we—and Nya—are meant to believe that Miranda is hapless but lovable, rather than insincere and self-serving.

Stephanie and I were on high alert in the first couple of episodes, evaluating whether the characters of color would be, as showrunner Michael Patrick King (2021) promised, richly developed with narrative arcs independent of the original cast. The end of the episode left Stephanie and me as skeptical as ever. Charlotte spent the episode scurrying around the Upper East Side trying to find a Black acquaintance to invite to her dinner party so her new friend Lisa wouldn't be the only Black person there. The big reveal at the end is that Lisa, too, had been concerned about inviting Charlotte and her husband to her party because they would be the only white people there. This reveal recast Charlotte's racist tokenism as, to quote myself in my exchange with Stephanie, "just like zany hijinks and lulz. like: 'oh silly char, you had nothing to worry about after all, LTW doesn't have any white friends either.'"

A Critical Engagement Framework

While our engagement with the show was certainly active, it was still in keeping with what the *SATC*-verse has always called on its audiences to do. As I posted my Stories, I couldn't help but wonder: can engaging with a pop culture text in a way that boosts interest in it ever truly be critical? Or does that engagement simply send everyone back into the same old consumerist loop?

Creative power, after all, is much more easily democratized than economic power. This sort of online chatter, after all, doesn't typically upend or even contest the most meaningful power structures at play in the *SATC* franchise. My Stories are among the show's paratexts, texts that both support interpretation of a central text (the show) and boost interest in it (Gray, 2010). You could see these Stories as a form of fanfiction in which I write myself and everyone I know into the show's cinematic universe.

History of Critical Literacy

In our *SATC* discourse, my friends and I were reaching for—though not consistently reaching—a state of critical engagement. I use the term *critical* here not in the sense of *critical thinking* or the commonplace sense of *criticizing*, or finding fault with, an object of study. My use of the term is rooted in Marx's (1932/2016) emphasis on interpreting how texts reflect economic and social structures. When we critically engage with a text, that text helps us understand something bigger about the world that produced it. Let's start with a brief (admittedly selective) history of *critical* in this sense.

In the classic text *Pedagogy of the Oppressed*, Brazilian educator Paolo Freire (1970) built the conceptual foundation of what would later become *critical pedagogy*. Freire called on educators to reject traditional models of education in which teachers knew things, students didn't, and the teacher's job was simply to "deposit" their knowledge into students. Freire derided this approach as the "banking model of education." To Freire, the project of education was to develop students' critical consciousness, an awareness of how power operates in society to oppress and marginalize, and to develop tools of resistance.

In this early work, Freire (1970) had his sights set on improving adult literacy programs in his native Brazil, not necessarily on revolutionizing educational practice. In the 1980s and 1990s, Henry Giroux, an American-Canadian cultural critic, broadened the scope of Freire's work. Like Freire, Giroux argued that education should empower and enable students to resist society's oppressive and dehumanizing forces. This form of education is what Giroux called *critical pedagogy*. Also like Freire, Giroux didn't see knowledge as something that resides in the mind of the teacher, but as something that's created collaboratively in the interactions between teacher and student (Giroux & Simon, 1988).

Giroux's work originated in but ultimately expanded Freire's approach. His approach was more sweeping; the goals he set for the critical pedagogue even loftier. In 2004, he wrote:

> As a critical practice, pedagogy's role lies not only in changing how people think about themselves and their relationship to others and the world, but also in energizing students and others to engage in those struggles that further possibilities for living in a more just society. (p. 63)

The branch of critical pedagogy most relevant to our discussion is *critical literacy*. While literacy is traditionally thought of as a set of processes happening in an individual's mind, critical literacy scholars saw it as a set of practices that happen in the world. In 1990, Luke and Freebody offered what would prove to be a durable framework for critical literacy scholars and practitioners: the Four Resources Model. The model describes four roles of readers: The reader as *code breaker* decodes texts. The reader as *text participant* uses background knowledge to make meaning of text. The reader as *text user* uses texts as part of purposeful activities in the social world. And, finally, the reader as *text analyst* takes a critical stance toward the text.

This final role, the *text analyst*, is most relevant to this discussion. The text analyst role is premised upon an understanding that "all texts are crafted objects, written by persons with particular dispositions or orientations toward the information, regardless of how factual or neutral the products may attempt to be" (p. 13). The text analyst, then, seeks to uncover the ideology of a text—even, or especially, texts that purport to have no ideology—and examines how power works within and through it. It was in defining this fourth role of a reader, theretofore overlooked in mainstream literacy programs, that Luke and Freebody articulated the premises, purposes, and practices involved in critical reading.

Applied to pop culture texts, critical literacy has shifted and expanded how we think about readers, texts, and culture. Early scholarship in critical literacy emphasizes the ways in which young people are vulnerable to hegemonic messages of pop culture. This body of work suggests that it's the educator's job to help them challenge and resist those messages. Critical literacy, then, is a method of correcting false consciousness.

In line with this view, Giroux (2004) proposed a way of thinking about pop culture as a form of *public pedagogy*, which he defined as "the diverse ways in which culture functions as a contested sphere over the production, distribution, and regulation of power, and how and where it operates both symbolically and institutionally as an educational, political, and economic force" (p. 65). To conceptualize pop culture as public pedagogy is to consider and account for the ways education happens through our engagement with it. In this view, pop culture is forceful in its influence over its audiences.

More recent critical literacy approaches account for and accommodate multiple, diverse, and even contradictory readings of pop culture texts and recognize that pop culture's influence isn't linear or predictable. In these approaches, the purpose of critical literacy is not simply to replace one reading of a text with a new, more enlightened reading of the text (Moeller, 2011). Scholars including Walkerdine (1990) and later Janks (2009),

Vasquez et al. (2019), and Morrell (2007) have shifted our focus away from the texts themselves and toward the dynamic and situated practices that are involved in the reading process. Like their forebears, these scholars looked for interpretive tools and pedagogical practices that could help young people challenge and resist hegemonic messages carried by those texts.

Key Concepts

As a conceptual framework, *critical literacy* has picked up many meanings, emphases, and applications over the course of its decades of travel through academic scholarship and everyday classroom practice. When it comes to our critical engagement with pop culture, I propose the following key concepts.

Texts are crafted objects. As Luke and Freebody (1990) put it, texts are "crafted objects." This framing emphasizes the crafted or constructed nature of texts. Individuals or groups of individuals made a series of choices to create something that didn't exist before. To critically read a text, we must first understand it as something that was deliberately created by human—or, increasingly, artificial—intelligence. I also begin with this premise to emphasize the breadth of what we, as critical readers, should count as a text. If a text is a crafted object, it is not simply a collection of printed words on a page or screen. A text can be a song, a meme, a TV show, a TikTok, a toy, a video game, a sports event. When we fail to recognize the textuality of such digital and physical objects, we miss much of the potential for criticality.

Because texts are crafted objects, they can never be neutral. Our common sense might tell us that some texts—say, a textbook chapter, a news article, instructions for assembling Swedish furniture—are more neutral, more objective, than others. But if we're going to move through our text-saturated world as critical readers, we need to at least recognize that all texts are ideological, even if, for practical reasons, we don't actively engage with them as such.

Texts are not closed systems. Recall what Stuart Hall (1980) called the "preferred reading" of a text (see Chapter 1): an individual author has a meaning in mind. The author encodes that meaning using semiotic systems in a text. Then, the reader decodes the text, and that meaning reproduces itself in the reader's mind. In this view, the text is a closed—airtight, even—system of moving meaning from the author's mind to the reader's mind. This view is how we get verbs like *contain*, *convey*, and *communicate* when we discuss a text's meanings and messages.

Like Hall (1980), I argue that texts don't simply *contain*, *convey*, and *communicate* meanings and messages to readers. I argue instead that they make certain meanings and messages *available* to readers. That means that texts—including pop culture texts—make certain ideas feel more or less legible, comprehensible, sensible, palatable, or appealing to readers. Texts don't control the meanings a reader makes of a text, but texts can facilitate the meaning-making process.

This is why, after a period of great effort and consternation, I've chosen the prepositions *within* and *through* to describe how power operates. Critical readers analyze how power operates *within* texts by observing how individual text elements operate together to encode meanings. But critical readers must also understand how texts are socially situated. How did the text come to exist? How and by whom was it created, disseminated, and consumed? Texts are inherently social objects. This means that, even if, ostensibly, a single human being created a text, that single human being created it from within a sociocultural context, using socially constructed resources.

Critical readers are self-aware. Before we can do anything else as critical readers, we must realize that what we are doing when we're reading is *reading*. We understand that any engagement with a text involves some form of active decoding (whether of language, imagery, sound, gesture) and meaning-making. We can't read critically if we don't know we're reading at all.

In addition to being self-aware about what we're doing, we're also self-aware about the knowledge we are bringing to the text and reflective about how that knowledge might shape what we notice, think, and understand through our engagement with the text. We're self-aware about our purposes for reading and engaging and how those purposes too might shape what we notice, think, and understand.

Finally, because critical readers aren't neutral, we must also be self-aware about the ideologies, biases, experiences, and identities that shape our engagement with texts. This self-awareness involves recognizing what we're carrying with us into the reading experience and tracing how these elements influence the texts we choose to engage with and how we choose to interpret and respond to them.

Critical readers don't mind contradiction. As critical readers, we don't strive to arrive at that one ultimate interpretation of a text. We're not looking to reach a state of critical enlightenment. There's no such endgame to critical reading. Instead, as critical readers, we relish the opportunity to reflect on how we're making meaning of texts and to engage with others. We recognize and celebrate the multiplicity of interpretation and the way meanings can shift over time.

And, importantly, we don't need to disapprove of or reject a text to read it critically. Critical readers see no need to put down joy and pick up criticality. We relish what the internet calls a *problematic fave*, a text we love despite its offenses, and a text we criticize despite our love for it. After all, loving something—being moved by it, feeling attached to it—can be a great place from which to be critical. Love, in that sense, can help us understand how the text operates, and how power operates within and through it.

Snapshots: Critical Engagement in Everyday Life

Critical Memeing

In late 2023, my corner of the internet was overrun by t-chart memes. This meme format presents two similar images under starkly contrasting headings. Some creators used this simple structure to comment on the ironies—and vagaries—of fashion's visual vocabulary. One example featured two versions of a typical workwear ensemble: camo trucker hat, Carhartt jacket, cowboy boots, and a beer bottle (patheticfashion, 2023). The version on the left is labeled "die liberal," and the version on the right, "slay queen." The "slay queen" version is tweaked ever so slightly: the jacket is sharper, the boots are snazzier, and the "die liberal" Budweiser is swapped out for a "slay queen" Bud Light. The "slay queen" version of the camo hat bears the slogan "God's Favorite." It's a signature piece from Praying—a brand I can only describe as an ouroboros of an enterprise, feeding on the revival of mid-aughts indie sleaze fashion that is its only basis for existence. The meme shows how clothes (and beers) traditionally coded as conservative and working class have been recast as trendy for and by a particular subset of queer urbanites.

The meme calls into question which of these two groups, working class conservatives or queer urbanites, is more powerful. On one hand, the more affluent urban queer consumer, who can afford the ironic trucker hat, has appropriated working class garb for their own expressive sartorial play ("blue collar cosplay," as Lauren Cochrane [2023], writing for *GQ*, put it). Yet this more affluent consumer is also, currently and as ever, under political attack by politicians who cater to the very group from which they've appropriated their sartorial signifiers. The meaning—and humor—of the meme lies in these sorts of dynamic, and irresolvable, contradictions.

But I argue that the meme, and others in this format, are doing more than playing in irony. They're highlighting the absurdity of consumerism itself. In this example, we have one legacy clothing brand, Carhartt, which has always, presumably with all due glee, accommodated shifts in its customer base, regardless of the political divisions between its factions (Cochrane, 2023). And we have Praying which, with their ironic, conservative-coded slogans, "transforms their simple creations into something more sinister, perverse, and wanted" (Satenstein, 2021). The meaning of the Carhartt jacket on the "slay queen" consumer is made intelligible by the layer of irony that the "God's Favorite" camo hat adds. One purchase necessitates another purchase.

Did *I* make this meaning of the meme, or did its creator? Recall that, in the critical engagement framework, texts aren't closed systems that simply encode and convey meaning. Texts are open signifying systems that make meanings *available* to readers. The meme makes my interpretation available, even if it doesn't predetermine it. Meme formats, repeated and reimagined across digital space over time, make meanings not just available but *readily* available. It took me nearly 400 words to explain the contradictions and ironies of this iteration of the format, whereas the meme makes these contradictions and ironies intelligible at a glance, at least to a knowing reader. The consumer goods the meme's creator references are also open systems. Clothes don't simply encode and convey meaning. As this meme highlights, sartorial codes shift over time and in response to human engagement. It's striking that a meme format as excruciatingly simple as a t-chart proves to be so well-suited to the task of encouraging critical engagement.

The in-and-out list is another meme format that invites critical engagement. This format is a take on the lists published by fashion magazines, which traditionally indicate the styles that should be cycled in or out for the coming season. The intention, quite plainly, is to stir up consumerist yearnings, to send customers running, or clicking, to the nearest retailer. At the turn of 2024, TikTokers repurposed the genre as new year's resolutions. The early creators who made a go of the format did so in personal, often funny, and occasionally critical ways.

Across these early iterations, many of which were posted by young women, several themes emerged (see Vi, 2023 and Lee, 2023):

- Self-care: "less than 7 hours of sleep" is out, and "sobriety" is in
- Anti-consumerism: "impulse purchasing" is out, and "outfit repeating" is in
- Setting boundaries, particularly with straight men: "being low maintenance" and "Gemini men" are both out; "putting your phone on Do Not Disturb" is in
- Body positivity: "unwarranted body commentary" and "assigning morality to weight"—both out
- Self-expression: "substack! writing! reveling in expression!"—in

Mixed into these themes were actual trend appraisals, in the traditional sense ("clean girl aesthetic" is out; "leopard prints, polka dots + sailor fashion" is in) and hyper-personal updates ("getting off birth control lol," also in).

Of course, I see evidence of critical engagement in the list items that push against consumerism, the unequal power dynamics of heterosexual relationships, and the pressure to be thin. But, more to the point, the act of reimagining this fundamentally consumerist genre and asserting oneself as a tastemaker of one's own life is critical too. The juxtaposition, and sometimes enmeshing, of the political and the personal in these lists suggests the multiplicity of the author's tastes, perspectives, and identities. The creators seem to be relishing the multiplicity and the contradictions of being human in a complicated social world.

I'll offer one more meme format—one that is truly after my own heart. As we've already seen, sharing pop culture interpretations and fan theories on social media is nothing new. In 2018, Amanda Yeo launched the perfect meme format for just such activity when she tweeted: "In the 1998 Disney film Mulan, Li Shang shuns Fa Mulan when he discovers that she is a woman because his attraction to her threatens his recent and hard-fought acceptance as a gay man. In this essay I will." Simply concluding a hot-take fan theory with the phrase "In this essay I will" is the whole format. Here's another early example from the Twitter account @scene-destroyer:

> The Dixie Chicks' bold declaration of their anti-war beliefs to an audience of ultra-conservative country fans, and refusal to apologize or back down in spite of death threats and plummeting sales makes them more punk than any band of straight men. In this essay I will. (2018)

According to Google trends (as cited on knowyourmeme.com, n.d.), the format gained interest over its first four years of existence and has since reached a high point of continued interest—earning its place in the meme format firmament, one might say. It's hard to imagine a more definitive example of critical engagement than the "In this essay I will" format. Yes, sometimes, these memes are just for kicks, finding humor in superimposing wildly convoluted theoretical frameworks on the pop culture texts least worthy of close examination. But, often, they present earnest critical analyses of pop culture, arguing that a given text either reinforces or counters hegemonic narratives and ideas. We see this in the two early examples I've shared here.

Why not simply write out the fan theory and post it? What does the phrase "in this essay I will" do for the fan in question? The phrase adds a touch of self-aware self-deprecation. It gives the fan tacit permission to nerd out, so to speak, over some aspect of a pop culture text that others might overlook. Adding "in this essay I will" is akin to saying, "Welcome to my TED talk." In the critical engagement framework, this sort of self-awareness is key. The creator of the meme knows not only *that* they're reading a text when they engage with pop culture but also *how* they're reading it. They know what knowledge, experiences, and, yes, theoretical frameworks they're bringing to the text. At the risk of overstating the power of this meme format, I'd suggest that the deep critic-ality on display in these memes would not be possible without the social cover the format provides for sharing nerdy, overwrought, hyper-intellectual interpretations of pop culture texts.

Critical Influencing

In June 2023, ahead of a possible initial public offering, the Chinese fast fashion company Shein invited influencers to tour its Guangzhou manufacturing facilities. Presumably, the company's intention was to quiet crescendoing accusations that the com-pany relies on forced labor to keep its prices low. The influencers obliged, posting videos gushing about the clean factories and comfortable working conditions. The accusations against Shein, however, hadn't been linked to the so-called "innovation centers" the influencers toured but to labor practices deeper in its supply chain (Romo, 2023).

Textile artist and content creator Elliot Rockart (2023) posted a TikTok mocking the influencers' posts. In the video, Rockart pretends to be an influencer invited to tour Greenwich Village's infamous Triangle Shirtwaist Factory, in which there was a ser-ious fire in March 1911, killing 146 garment workers, most of them immigrant girls and women. As the fire broke out, workers couldn't escape because the stairwells and exits had been locked, a common practice intended to prevent workers from taking unauthorized breaks and stealing.

In the characteristic sing-songy cadence of a fashion influencer, Rockart narrates their "visit" to the Triangle Shirtwaist Factory:

I'm a Triangle Shirtwaist ambassador here in New York getting a closer look behind the scenes at the Triangle Shirtwaist Factory here in Greenwich village. I loved getting to learn about each step of the manufacturing process, as well as actually seeing the working conditions for myself. Like many others, I've heard a lot of misinformation, so I enjoyed seeing it firsthand. There are lots of stairs and exits in case of emergency, and they use a lot of technology which puts less work on the workers. I also loved getting to know all the people here on the Triangle Shirtwaist team. I'm so thankful for Triangle Shirtwaist for all the opportunities it's given to me and others. (2023)

As Rockart narrates the visit, they superimpose video of themself mugging like an influencer: a flirtatious hunch forward, a tilt of the chin, a kick of the heel, a coy eye roll, and a blown kiss to top it off. The video of Rockart is overlaid on historical photographs of the factory's cramped workrooms and burned-out stairwells.

The video operates as both parody and satire. As a parody, it sends up the genre of fashion influencer content. Specifically, it highlights how vapid the genre can be, how out of touch it is with the material concerns of the so-called real world, and how the genre requires influencers to smush their whole selves and their whole lives into the recognizable shape of "content." As satire, the video uses the ironic juxtaposition of cheery influencer content and unsettling photographs of labor abuses to expose the mechanisms of the influencer economy that sustains fast fashion companies like Shein. Influencers after all require an endless supply of new clothes to push their young audiences to buy. Rockart's sing-songy cadence is what it sounds like when an influencer reads—but tries to sound like they're not reading—a script. Their cadence, along with the four mentions of the "brand's" name, remind us who's in whose pockets in this economy: they're both in each other's (very cheaply constructed) pockets.

It's worth noting that the comments are critical in their own right. @mistresspennywhistle commented, "Omg people are so quick to assume the worst, their shirtwaists are FIRE," followed by three fire emojis. @kittenmittons said, "Can't wait for my next shirt-waist haul! So great to know supporting the TSF has no ramifications whatsoever." @caet22 noted that "the fire escape plan looks very thought out and efficient, putting my application in rn!!" And @Kristinlee_p732 enthused, "They don't even lock their workers in the factory, but I wanted to be locked in because it was so lux-urious!" There were also several history teachers in the comments praising the video and suggested they might use it in their class.

In the critical engagement framework, texts are crafted objects. The pop culture texts worth examining in this case include Rockart's TikTok, the influencer genre it parodies, the comment section, and the actual clothes that Shein, along with its band of obliging influencers, sells. But the garments themselves are the center of this entire signifying system. Shein's garments hold the whole history of the style trends that make them appealing, the media apparatuses that make them popular, and the labor practices that make them cheap. Rockart's critical reading of these garments pulls in all three of these elements. They read the garments as texts that have been crafted in a particular way for a particular reason. And, in a 39-second TikTok, they illuminate the garments' buried meanings, which could potentially shift how their viewers think about what they wear.

Critical Engagement in the Classroom

Critical Engagement Up Close

To illustrate the potential of critical engagement in the classroom, I offer two passages of conversation. The first is not very critical at all—by my, or anyone's, definition. I open with this conversa-tion to put the second in relief. The conversations illustrate two diametric reading stances, or ways of relating to, interpreting, and responding to a text. The first, what I call an *endostory* stance, is one in which the reader enters the world of the story, treating the characters as real people. When a reader takes an endostory stance, their interpretations and responses focus on the highs and lows of characters' experiences, as well as their inner thoughts, feelings, and motivations.

The second, an *exostory* stance, is one in which the reader treats the story like the crafted object it is. An exostory interpretation addresses why and how a text was made and how it is constructed to convey particular meanings and messages. To put it another way, when we take an endostory stance, we're pulled into the narrative world; when we take an exostory stance, we're pulled out of it.

The Endostory Stance

Week three of Group, it was just me, Kaylee, Audrey, and Briana. I'd lost Danielle and Jasmine to the jubilant chaos of a teacher–student basketball game put on as a reward for upper school students in the last period of the day. The four of us watched an episode of *Black-ish* (Barris et al., 2017), a popular sitcom about a Black family living in a wealthy, predominantly white suburb of Los Angeles, grappling with personal and sociopolitical issues. The episode we watched served as a backdoor pilot of *Grown-ish*, a spinoff that follows the character Zoey, played by Yara Shahidi, in college.

In the episode, Zoey attends orientation and befriends Miriam. By way of a platonic meet-cute, the two characters excuse themselves to the restroom in unison after the small-group leader invites everyone to introduce themselves and say how they'd like to be identified. (Stacy is a "tri-racial gender-fluid, panoramic [sic] demisexual" whose pronoun is *they*.") Zoey and Miriam quickly bond over their shared aversion to the rigmarole of orientation: the expectation of oversharing, the hyper-specific interest groups, and the try-hard administrators.

Early in the episode, they meet Aaron, the attractive leader of the Black Student Union. Aaron recruits Zoey to join the BSU and, in keeping with the conventions of the genre, Zoey, tongue-tied over his attractiveness, proceeds to embarrass herself in front of Aaron in this and several more scenes over the course of the episode. In the second act, Aaron asks Zoey and Miriam if they want to check out the dorms. Zoey, by this point fully lovestruck, murmurs, "Yeah, I'd go anywhere with you." She then makes a feeble attempt to save face, Aaron steps away, and Zoey asks Miriam, "Why didn't you stop me?" Miriam replies, "I didn't want to. It was funny."

That's where our conversation begins. I asked the group what they thought brought Miriam and Zoey together as friends and what the show might be saying about friendship between young women. Briana offered that the characters recognized a similar kind of weirdness in each other when they both "[tried] to get out of the situation." Audrey picked up on Briana's claim that they were weird, but pivoted to the later scene:

> **Audrey**: I feel like the white girl, she's kinda weird like how Briana said. . . . You can't just like—How [Zoey] slipped when she was talking to the boy. Zoey asked her, "Why didn't you stop me?" and [Miriam] said, "It was funny." That's kind of mean.
>
> **Briana**: Sometimes friends do that.
>
> **Kaylee**: Sometimes, yeah.
>
> **Briana**: Like she [Kaylee] does that.
>
> **Kaylee**: Are you serious?!
>
> **Mia [to Briana]**: You let your friend embarrass herself because you think it's gonna be funny?
>
> **Kaylee**: Or, like, probably so because she learns a lesson not to say something like that ever again to somebody.

At this point, it was clear that there was no stopping this story:

> **Briana**: So this boy asked me out yesterday.
>
> **Kaylee**: Yesterday?
>
> **Briana**: Justin.
>
> **Kaylee**: Oh, yeah. But she was very shy about it, so I got—
>
> **Briana**: Shy?! Shy?!
>
> **Kaylee**: Like, "You better go out with her, you better go out with her now." Yes, you were shy.
>
> **Briana**: I don't want to go into that. I don't want to go up to [boys] and be like, "You go out with me." I would expect the guy asking the girl out.
>
> **Kaylee**: He already did!
>
> **Audrey**: That relates to um, when she [Zoey] was nervous because she wanted to say—

Kaylee: Yeah, she said that he was cute, but, at the end, she loves him. I wanna watch another episode to see how that relationship is gonna go.

Briana wasn't ready to cede control of the conversation quite yet.

Briana: I think we were going somewhere. I don't know, but I think it was with the school. We were going somewhere, and I like this boy, and me and him were talking and everything—
Kaylee: She always says random stuff.
Briana: I say mad random stuff, and the guy was like [rolls eyes].
Kaylee: I think he was pretending to listen. I think he was confused with what you were saying.
Briana: He was mad confused and then Kaylee was like, "Oh my god, this is so funny!" And I was like, "How come you didn't stop me? How come you didn't protect me? I made a total fool of myself." And she was like, "I don't know, I just thought it was funny?"

I tried to gently steer the conversation back toward analytical ground, asking if this is a good or bad thing about female friendship. Audrey, Briana, and Kaylee all saw both good and bad elements.

Audrey: It's kinda good and bad. It's good because it's funny, and you're learning a lesson, and then it's bad because, like, I don't think you wanna embarrass yourself.
Briana: Yeah.
Kaylee: And I think kinda good because you're letting yourself be more open to people and not just like you're so scared.
Briana: Um, yeah, but I think it might be bad sometimes because if you just met the girl, and you guys are not really that close—You think that she might be stabbing your back or that she don't like you or something because she's not protecting you in that moment. And you expect someone to protect you. But in the other case, if you're making a total fool of yourself, you might learn a lesson.

To Audrey, Briana, and Kaylee, it is through everyday social interaction that people "learn lessons" about how to act. Friends serve to define what is appropriate, expected, and normal indirectly (by allowing consequences of inappropriate action to unfold of their own accord) or directly (by intervening or teasing each other). In this framework, a friend's embarrassment is, perhaps, a small price to pay for the lesson of how to act normal—how to fit in.

The conversation here zigzagged between the episode and their own lives. Even though their conversation veered out of the story and into their personal lives, I argue that Audrey, Briana, and Kaylee are taking up a definitively *endostory* stance. They're engaging with and interpreting the episode as if Zoey, the fictional character, is someone they know. They're judging her and her friend Miriam for their actions, just as they'd judge people they know (including each other). They're not interested in what point the show's screenwriters, directors, and actors are trying to make about female friendships or heteroromantic relationships. And they're certainly not questioning or contesting the ideas that the show's creators made available.

Is there critical possibility in endostory readings? The girls did not simply reconstruct the story on a literal level, approximating the story the creators of the show intended to tell. Instead, in line with the tenets that neither critical readers nor texts are neutral, they brought their own experiences and understandings to bear on their interpretation of the story, and they used the story as a framework to understand their own lives. The missing piece here is, I argue, self-awareness. Imagine what might be possible if, as teachers, we built self-awareness into this conversation, inviting young people to consider *why* they feel pulled into this text and whether there are patterns in the texts that have this effect on us. What kinds of stories create narrative worlds that feel like extensions of our own? How do our experiences shape our interpretations of these stories, and how do our interpretations shape the sense we make of our experiences?

In my experience, endostory readings are pleasurable. It's only possible to take an endostory stance if the text has already been successful in transporting you into its world. And it can be fun to talk about characters like they're people we know—a guilt-free form of gossip. An educator's goal, I think, shouldn't be to move young people away from the delights of an endostory reading.

It would be to move them into a place of contradiction and simultaneity, a place from which they can both enjoy *and* critically analyze the text.

The Exostory Stance

Two weeks later, the full group was back. From their list of favorite artists, I'd selected a few music videos to watch. We started with A Boogie's "Timeless" (2016). In the video, shots of A Boogie and his friends are spliced with shots of two women in black strappy leotards dancing in silhouette against shifting hot pink, purple, and blue backdrops. The video has no narrative elements—that is, nothing happens in the video—aside from a few stray shots of A Boogie and his friends walking down a city street and A Boogie smoking marijuana.

When the video ended and we brought the lights back up, Jasmine jumped right in: "Okay, so the girl? She was dressed very, very inappropriate—her clothes is all like strings." The group agreed, and she added that her dancing looked "like a fish swimming in water. . . no other human dances like that." I asked Jasmine why she might be dancing like that, and she made no bones about it: "to reveal herself."

"And trying to be sexy," Kaylee added, as Briana re-enacted the dance, sucking her cheeks in to look like a fish. Getting serious, she shifted the conversation into analysis:

> Her clothes were tight and what she was doing looked like she was trying to be high, but I think she was doing that on purpose because it made the girl look like she's like a side chick because he was like you know grinding. . . . The girl, I mean, she was dancing, like everything was popped out. When you dance, you don't dance like that. Anyway, her clothes were way too tight. . . . She was wearing some type of panties where you could see the skin go pop and everything. Like, girl, put some pants out—put some pants on!

Kaylee drew our attention to the song's lyrics, which I'd printed out for them. "The lyrics were a bit too much because it was calling the girl a 'b' and a side chick and stuff like that. That's so inappropriate."

Kaylee's shift in focus from image to language brought about an ever bigger a shift: the group began to shift the blame for the video's "inappropriateness" from the women to A Boogie. They made it clear that boys and men are the ones who refer to women as "side bitches" (euphemized as "side chicks").

"We get called all these names by boys," Kaylee said, aligning herself with the women in the video who are made out to be side chicks.

"So what does it mean to be a side chick or a side bitch? What does that mean?" I asked.

According to Kaylee, Jasmine, and Briana, a side chick is:

Kaylee: You're just like, you know—
Jasmine: The other one—
Briana: You're not—
Jasmine: You're the one after the main.
Briana: He has the main. She's just the side one.
Jasmine: She's the other one.

This pieced-together definition emphasizes that a side chick is a position, not an identity. It's a position that defined by what one is not ("the main"), where one falls in the man's hierarchy ("after"), and one's insignificance as an individual ("the other one").

The *side chick* exchange wound up activating the latent criticality of the discussion. The group began talking about the dancers, not as doers, but as objects of others' doing. Briana, dancing in her seat and improvising a melody for emphasis, said that the dancers were "told to do that to get paid."

> **Jasmine**: It's kind of showing the girl as being inferior because of what he's making her do, like being a side person. He's saying stuff bad about her like he can boss her into doing what he wants to do. When it comes to her wanting to do something, she can't do it.
> **Kaylee**: They don't like it, but they do it. They earn money for it, for example, to provide for their families. They will do anything for their families.
> **Briana**: I think that she might like doing this because A Boogie is all the way up there because he's rich and all famous

and everything . . . now he's making money because of his music . . . and now those two girls should probably do it because . . . it might make them famous or something. I don't know—make them recognizable and make the managers or the directors choose them to do other videos with other like singers and everything.

Jasmine: They do it because that's their job.

In this exchange, the girls echoed each other's points, emphasizing the power differences between the rich and famous men who make choices and the women who carry out those choices.

Later, Audrey suggested that Black women are uniquely subjected to pressure to alter their appearance to please straight men. She explained, "White people . . . have everything. They have a pathway out but a Black person—a Black woman . . . [has] to work way harder to get what they want in life, what they want to achieve."

In these discussions, the girls' critique of the powerful-man amalgam is not always explicit. However, they described how he constricts the less-powerful-woman amalgam's choices, exploiting her financial need. While their earliest comments are tinged with judgment, they eventually take what they're seeing in this text and use it to illustrate just how far women, and particularly Black women, will go to provide for their children and advance their career. In this discussion, they criticize the systems of power involved in producing hyper-sexualized images of Black women in music videos.

The protagonists in this invented story are recognizable as mothers who "will do anything" for their families. If there are villains in this narrative, they are A Boogie and the other presumably male producers and directors who make women appear as they do. Yet, aside from Briana's concern that little boys watch these videos and see them as a model of how to treat women, the girls don't totally vilify the men. The heterosexual male interest in presenting women as objects of desire is treated as fact in the girls' story. The protagonists are forgiven their inappropriateness because they did what needed to be done in the face of this fact.

Audrey's and Briana's comments could be understood as *probable stories* (see Chapter 1). They improvise and encode a story of the dancers' lives to interpret and decode their appearance in the video. I also take their comments to illustrate two critical engagement concepts. First, while Audrey and Briana improvised a story, they didn't invent it from scratch. The story has recognizable features. Søndergaard (2002) offered the term *storylines* to describe recognizable stories of indeterminate origin:

> The term *storyline* refers to a course of events, a sequence of actions that . . . creates identities through inclusive and exclusive discursive movements, a naturalized and conventional cultural narrative, one that is often used as the explanatory framework of one's own and others' practices and sequences of action. (p. 191)

Storylines are recycled in cultural texts and, through this recycling, circulate taken-for-granted messages and meanings. The girls' story of the mother who sacrifices herself by doing sexualized labor to provide for her family is a storyline that reinforces ideas about respectability, heterosexual femininity, and motherhood. According to the logic of this storyline, the woman is doing a kind of work that would mark her as disreputable. She is redeemed, however, because she does this work toward her highest purpose, to fulfill her most important role, as a mother.

Second, the characters in Audrey's and Briana's stories—A Boogie and the dancers—are also recognizable. *Character tropes* are the naturalized, conventional figures in stories like these. We need only understand a few details about the character—and indeed Audrey and Briana know very little about them—to extrapolate their entire inner and outer worlds. For example, all we know about the dancers is what they wear and how they dance in the video. From there, the group extrapolated the dynamics of their relationship with A Boogie, their professional and personal motivations, their experiences of societal and financial pressure, and the inner conflict that comes with managing a constrained set of choices. They're able to flesh out this character precisely because the mother who will do anything to provide for her children is a recognizable figure in our cultural narratives.

Critical engagement requires self-awareness, and self-awareness, I'd suggest, requires language. Young people must be able to articulate and discuss how they're making meaning of texts. Audrey, Briana, and the others *know* about storylines and character tropes in the sense that they're tapping into them in their discussions. But they are developing the language to describe—and to negotiate—what they know could move them into a deeper level of criticality.

Endostory and Exostory Key Points

- ◆ When we take an endostory stance, we get swept up in the story. We think of the characters just as we think of real people, empathizing with them, evaluating their actions, and rooting for particular outcomes for them.
- ◆ When we take an exostory stance, we step back from the text and analyze it as a constructed object. We consider how and why the text is constructed as it is, noting the different people who made choices about the text and the larger sociocultural context from which they made those choices.

Teaching Possibilities

The critical engagement framework tells us that, to help young people engage more critically with texts, we must cultivate their self-awareness as critical readers, allow them to dwell in contradictory stances and interpretations, and help them to see that texts are constructed objects that exist within larger sociocultural systems. Table 2.1 offers some initial ideas for supporting students in becoming more critical in interpreting, responding to, and even composing texts. While Chapters 4–6 offer full lessons, these ideas can be dropped into any class, especially English classes, without much preparation.

TABLE 2.1 Supporting critical interpretation, response, and composition in the classroom.

Interpretation

Endostory	Exostory
Affirm students' instincts and desires to interpret and evaluate characters' thoughts, words, and actions, as we would interpret and evaluate real people's thoughts, words, and actions. Nudge students to develop self-awareness about their endostory readings: ♦ Invite them to reflect on the aspects of their identities, experiences, social-emotional understandings, and values they bring to bear on their interpretations of a text ♦ Invite them to reflect on the patterns of texts that do and don't pull them into an endostory stance	Support students in developing language and conceptual understandings that can help them become more astute interpreters of text. Consider teaching them the terms like *endostory, exostory, storyline,* and *character trope.* Encourage students to wonder: ♦ Who or what was involved in crafting this text? ♦ Who or what shaped the content and structure of this text? ♦ Who or what approved, or greenlit, this text for publication or distribution? ♦ Who or what was responsible for deciding how, when, and by whom this text would be read? As they reflect on these questions, guide students to recognize that all texts exist in a complex, multilayered sociocultural context and to interpret how power operates through the text.

Response

Endostory	Exostory
Create opportunities for students to put themselves in characters' shoes and discuss and debate multiple courses of action for the characters. Invite students to discuss what characters should or shouldn't do based on different frameworks: ♦ What's in the character's best interest? ♦ What course of action would best match the character's values? My values?	As you would in any literary analysis discussion, pose questions about how texts are constructed. Isolate specific aspects of the text and address how they work together to develop meaning. Nudge students to push beyond the assumption that the only meaning worth understanding is what the author intended. Invite students to consider the bigger sociocultural context that produced the text, not just the individual author.

(Continued)

TABLE 2.1 (Continued)

Response

Endostory	Exostory
◆ What would be the most ethical or just course of action? ◆ What would be the most emotionally healthy course of action?	Support students in identifying and discussing the biases, assumptions, ideologies, and value systems that work within and through the text.

Composition

Endostory	Exostory
Create opportunities for students to compose fanfiction that takes place in the narrative world of the text. For example: ◆ Students write their own storylines for the characters in their favorite movies or TV shows. ◆ Students write their own storylines for the characters in a literary text they're studying in school. ◆ Students write accounts of historical events from different figures' or groups' perspectives. ◆ Students write alternative histories as if a historical event hadn't happened or had turned out differently.	Create opportunities for students to compose criticism of all kinds of texts—pop culture and academic—in the style of contemporary pop culture criticism. For example: ◆ Students recap TV episodes, movies, or literary texts in the style of a *Vulture* or *A.V. Club* recap (see Chapter 4). These recaps layer interpretation, humor, and context into summaries of important plot points. ◆ Create a podcast episode (see Chapter 4) in which they discuss and debate how the text was constructed and what it means with a partner or small group. ◆ Create their own reaction videos that layer their own moment-to-moment reactions over an audio or video text. ◆ Compose a parody of a text that humorously comments on the text, genre, or format through exaggeration or recontextualization.

Exercises for Teachers

Interpretation Exercises

Reflect on the following:

◆ As you engage with a text, take note of your stance. Are you reading the text using an endostory or exostory stance?

♦ If you're taking an endostory stance, what aspects of your identity, experiences, social-emotional understandings, and/or values are you bringing to bear on your interpretation of the characters?

♦ If you're taking an exostory stance, notice your point of focus. Are you mostly analyzing and appreciating the way the author(s) constructed the text? Or are you critically evaluating how power operates within and through it?

Once you've recognized your stance, prompt yourself to take the opposite stance. Reflect:

♦ Does a shift in stance bring about a shift in feelings?

♦ Do you enjoy your "natural" stance more or less?

Reflect on patterns in the texts that pull you into the narrative and those that push you out of the narrative. Are there specific narrative moments, texts, or genres that tend to pull you in or push you out? What might explain those patterns?

Response Exercises

Choose a pop culture text that has been on your mind and respond to it either online or in in-person discussion with someone. Whether online or in person, track the stances you and others are taking over the course of the discussion.

♦ Are you and others discussing the text taking an endostory or exostory stance?

♦ If the discussion stance is endostory, notice your point of focus. For example, are you trying to understand the characters' interior lives, or are you judging their exterior words and actions?

♦ If the discussion stance is exostory, notice your point of focus. Are you mostly analyzing and appreciating the way the author(s) constructed the text? Or are you critically evaluating how power operates within and through the text?

Composition Exercises

Use pop culture tools to compose a text that captures something meaningful, interesting, or funny about your life. Share with others (privately or on social media—it's up to you!). For example:

- ◆ Select a pop culture text that stuck with you and compose your own parody that comments on the text's genre, structure, or content—find a way to share it with someone!
- ◆ Select a pop culture text that intrigues you and film your own reaction video. In the video, verbalize your endostory and exostory reactions to the text—find a way to share it with someone!

Final Note: Don't Take Anything for Granted

Critical engagement means not taking anything for granted. In the opening of this chapter, I cited critic Megan Garber's description of how pop culture texts can produce meaning: men invent categories, and women are expected to slot themselves into them. This phrasing comes from her essay on the 1989 romcom *When Harry Met Sally* (Reiner, 1989). While I'd seen it, I didn't know until I read Garber's piece that the film was responsible for introducing the concept of the "high-maintenance" woman. One night, Harry and Sally are talking on the phone in their separate beds as they both watch *Casablanca*. "There are two kinds of women: high-maintenance and low-maintenance," Harry explains. Ingrid Bergman, he says, is low-maintenance, while Sally is high-maintenance.

I'd given the same level of regard and critical thought to this way of categorizing women as I do to the air I breathe. Which is to say, none. And yet the image of the high-maintenance woman is pervasive. I can call to mind at least two separate sitcom b-stories from the 1990s that hinged on the idea that a character was high-maintenance. (The high-maintenance woman even makes an appearance in a 2024 meme I analyze in Chapter 3.) Texts present such ideas, and, when we're not looking, these ideas become fact.

Critical engagement means not taking anything for granted. I've been seeing a lot of memes about quicksand. These memes, which are quite clearly by and for elder Millennials, muse about how, as children, we were led to believe that quicksand would be a much bigger danger, a much bigger part of our lives, than it wound up being. For me, that's true. But how did it happen? I think there was an action-adventure movie (or two) from the 1980s that featured quicksand, and perhaps there was some quicksand involved in *Super Mario Bros. 2* (1988). That might have been enough for an entire generation (or so the memes would have you believe) to take for granted that quicksand would be a major problem in our lives.

Critical engagement means not taking anything for granted. Recently, I asked ChatGPT to generate some simple sentences that children can relate to. I was designing a first-grade lesson on sentence structure, and I wanted some examples to play around with. Regeneration after regeneration, it gave me sentences about puppies in yards fetching red balls on a sunny day. Apparently, this is what ChatGPT thinks childhood is.

In these contexts, AI averages out and flattens human experience, which, in many ways, is what the culture industries have always done. The categories become character tropes, the character tropes become characters, and the characters become how we understand people. Mere seconds after Harry introduced the low-maintenance/high-maintenance categories, he'd already abbreviated "low-maintenance" as "L-M." Its naturalization was already underway.

AI stands to supercharge the culture industries' ability to reinforce the categories we've invented and the logic we use to make sense of the world. If we let it, it will dull our feel for specifics and our appetite for counter-narratives. This is why critical engagement matters. Rather than letting texts tells us what is and what could be, we decide for ourselves.

References

[@scene-destroyer]. (2018, May 17). *The Dixie Chicks' bold declaration of their anti-war beliefs to an audience of ultra-conservative country fans, and refusal to apologize or back down* [Post]. X.

Barris, K., Wilmore, L., & Taylor, Y. (Writers). Griffiths, J. (Director). (2017, May 3). Liberal arts (Season 3, Episode 23) [TV series episode]. In A. Anderson, K. Barris, E. B. Dobbins, L. Fishburne, J. Groff, C. Nickerson, P. Principato, H. Sugland, & P. Young (Producers), *Black-ish*. ABC Studios.

Cochrane, L. (2023, January 25). The curious case of the sudden Carhartt boom. *GQ.* www.gq-magazine.co.uk/fashion/article/carhartt-brand-trend

A Boogie Wit Da Hoodie. (2016). *A Boogie Wit Da Hoodie—Timeless (DJ SPINKING)* [Video]. www.youtube.com/watch?v=zGzplqC5zvQ.

Fairless, C., & Garroni, L. (2019). *We should all be Mirandas: Life lessons from* Sex and the City's *most underrated character*. Dey Street Books.

Fairless, C., & Garroni, L. (Hosts). (2021–present). *Every outfit* [Audio podcast]. www.everyoutfitinc.com/

Freire, P. (1970). *Pedagogy of the oppressed*. Continuum.

Garber, M. (2019, July 19). The quiet cruelty of *When Harry Met Sally*. *The Atlantic.* www.theatlantic.com/entertainment/archive/2019/07/when-harry-met-sally-and-the-high-maintenance-woman/594382/

Giroux, H. A. (2004). Cultural studies, public pedagogy, and the responsibility of intellectuals. *Communication and Critical/Cultural Studies, 1*(1), 59–79.

Giroux, H. A., & Simon, R. I. (1988). Critical pedagogy and the politics of popular culture. *Cultural Studies, 2*(3), 294–320.

Gray, J. (2010). *Show sold separately: Promos, spoilers, and other media paratexts*. NYU Press.

Hall, S. (1980). Encoding/decoding. In S. Hall, D. Hobson, A. Lowe, & P. Willis (Eds.), *Culture, Media, Language* (pp. 128–138). Routledge.

Janks, H. (2009). *Literacy and power*. Routledge.

King, M. (Producer). (2021–present). *And just like that . . .* [TV series]. HBO Max.

King, M. (Host). (2021). *And just like that . . . the writer's room* [Audio podcast]. HBO Max.

knowyourmeme.com (n.d*.) In this essay I will.* https://knowyourmeme.com/memes/in-this-essay-i-will

Lee, M. [@oldloserinbrooklyn]. (2023, December 31). HYNE from OLIB [Post]. Instagram.

Luke, A., & Freebody, P. (1990). Literacies programs: Debates and demands in cultural context. *Prospect: An Australian Journal of TESOL, 5*(7), 7–16.

Marx, K., & Engels, F. (1932/2016). *The German ideology.* International Publishers.

Moeller, R. A. (2011). "Aren't these boy books?": High school students' readings of gender in graphic novels. *Journal of Adolescent & Adult Literacy, 54*(7), 474–486.

Morrell, E. (2007). *Critical literacy and urban youth.* Routledge.

patheticfashion. (2023, December 21). slay liberal [Post]. Instagram.

Reiner, R. (Director). (1989). *When Harry met Sally* [Film]. Columbia Pictures.

Robespierre, G. (Director). (2021). Some of my best friends (Season 1, Episode 4) [TV series episode]. In *And just like that. . . .* HBO Max.

Rockart, E. [@myweeklyyarn]. (2023, June 26). Surely this collab will have no consequences for me or any of the real #sheinfactory workers [Video]. TikTok.

Romo, V. (2023, June 30). Shein invited influencers on an all-expenses-paid trip. Here's why people are livid. *NPR.* www.npr.org/2023/06/30/1184974003/shein-influencers-china-factory-trip-backlash

Satenstein, L. (2021, November 30). Praying is the fashion industry's most perverse viral hit. *Vogue.* www.*vogue.*com/article/praying-label-skylar-newman-alex-haddad

Søndergaard, D. M. (2002). Poststructuralist approaches to empirical analysis. *International Journal of Qualitative Studies in Education, 15*(2), 187–204.

Star, D. (Producer). (1998–2004). *Sex and the city* [TV series]. HBO.

Vasquez, V. M., Janks, H., & Comber, B. (2019). Critical literacy as a way of being and doing. *Language arts, 96*(5), 300–311.

Vi [@vvicecelia]. (2023, December 17). personal ins and outs hehehe #2024 [Post]. TikTok.

Walkerdine, V. (1990). *Schoolgirl fictions.* Verso Books.

Yeo, A. [@amandamyeo]. (2018, March 7). *In the 1998 Disney film Mulan, Li Shang shuns Fa Mulan when he discovers that she is a woman* [Post]. X. https://x.com/amandamyeo/status/971506184027914240

3

Strategic Engagement

As I write this, I'm wearing two friendship bracelets made of plastic letter beads. They've been bothering me a bit—clicking against my laptop as I type—but I won't take them off. One reads, "meet me behind the mall," and the other, "florals for spring." Right away, I've divided you. Some know what these phrases mean; some don't. Some know why I, a full-grown Millennial adult, am wearing beaded friendship bracelets; some don't.

I made the first bracelet myself, but I'd be remiss not to add that I made it under the tutelage of a very cool third-grader named Catie. Catie is what's called a *Swiftie*, a fan of Taylor Swift. Like many Swifties in the era of the wildly successful *Eras* tour of 2023 and 2024, Catie has taken to making friendship bracelets. Swifties made and traded these bracelets at the *Eras* concerts, blanketing social media with photos of stacks of letter beads and messily braided threads on their wrists (Wind, 2024). Some attribute the practice to a lyric from the song "You're on Your Own, Kid" that encourages the listener to make friendship bracelets as a way of embracing the moment (Swift & Antonoff, 2022).

This is all to say that making friendship bracelets is a perfectly normal, perfectly intelligible Friday night activity for an

DOI: 10.4324/9781032667027-5

elder Millennial and her Gen Alpha buddy. Catie made me a thread bracelet of blue, purple, and pink (she vetoed my choice of red), and she instructed me to make my own letter bead bracelet based on my favorite Taylor Swift lyric. Without giving it a second thought, I chose "meet me behind the mall" from the song "August" (Swift & Antonoff, 2020). The lyric makes me nostalgic: nostalgic for malls themselves and for malls as an enabling setting of the adolescent clandestine. It reminds me of all the things I did in, around, and behind malls that I didn't want my parents to know about. I also happen to like the way these lyrics wrap around the melody at this moment of resolution in the song. So *meet me behind the mall*, it was.

The second bracelet is a more recent addition, and its origin story is more circuitous. I'll whiz through the details (some of which you may recall from Chapter 2): Chelsea Fairless and Lauren Garroni created @everyoutfit, an Instagram account that documented Carrie Bradshaw's best outfits from *Sex and the City* and offered commentary, in the pair's signature droll style, on the show's cultural significance; in 2021, *Every Outfit* became a podcast, part *Sex and the City* rewatch and part pop culture and fashion commentary.

A fan of the series, the Instagram account, and the podcast, I attended Fairless and Garroni's live show in early 2024. Fairless, a known Swiftie, and her wife made letter bead bracelets for the audience. At their show, the bracelets were passed around on a binder ring. Their messages ranged from podcast in-jokes, to famous *SATC* quotes, to references to adjacent pop culture properties. My choice, "florals for spring," was deadpanned by Meryl Streep as Miranda Priestly in the film *The Devil Wears Prada* (Frankel, 2006). (I can't help but mentally fill in the next word of Streep's line: *groundbreaking*.) *The Devil Wears Prada* shares some cultural DNA with *SATC*: it's a fashion movie, as *SATC* is a fashion show, and they shared a costume designer, Patricia Field.

This chapter is about strategic engagement, about how we actively choose to practice literacy in a pop-mediated world. When it comes to pop culture literacy, reading and writing aren't such distinct activities. My personal story of clandestine meetings helped me *read* the lyric "meet me behind the mall." But then that very lyric helped me write my own present-day story of self. My personal orientation against clichéd fashion motifs like "florals for spring" helped me interpret Streep's deadpan line-read. But then that very line-read helped me write—reinscribe and rearticulate—that attitude. In making the first bracelet and choosing the second, I import dozens of layers of meaning, personal and textual, into my sartorial self-expression. Yes, I made sense of what these words mean in their native contexts. But what's much more interesting to our discussion of strategic engagement is that I then appropriated these scraps of language into my own expression, my own encoding of self.

A Strategic Engagement Framework

This chapter addresses the third and final part of the pop culture literacy framework: strategic engagement. Previously, I illustrated how young people engage in pop culture *actively* and *critically* and suggested some ways we might extend their active and critical pop culture literacy practices. I conceptualize *strategic* engagement in pop culture texts just as I'd conceptualize it in relation to any other text. To read printed text strategically, a reader approaches the text with a clearly defined purpose, monitors their movement through the text toward that purpose, and modulates their way of reading to help them achieve it (these practices align to "active self-regulation," as defined by Duke & Cartwright, 2021).

If we're to import the concept of *strategic reading* into a discussion of pop culture, the strategies in question must be suited to the distinctive characteristics of pop culture texts and the digital environments in which we engage with them. *Multimodality* and *intertextuality* characterize both. In the Introduction, I described the waning and fragmentation of the so-called monoculture: beginning with the proliferation of cable TV channels in the 1990s; continuing with the rise of streaming services, social media, and smartphones in the 2000s; and, it stands to reason, proceeding ad infinitum with the explosive development of AI. Over the past century, culture moved from the public spaces of the cinema and the dancehall to the private spaces of our homes and, finally, to the devices in our hands.

Today, as we engage with pop culture in our homes, our attention is often split between our phones and our TVs. As journalist Delia Cai described the phenomenon in a 2020 tweet: "[A]nother day of staring at the big screen while scrolling through my little screen so as to reward myself for staring at the medium screen all week." Today, our pop culture *reading* doesn't have a distinct beginning, middle, and end. Our feeds are continuous (and endless, to boot), our attention is fragmented across multiple planes, and the origins and meanings of texts are, to say the least, ambiguous. To read these texts strategically, we must understand the way these texts make meanings available through multiple, interlocking semiotic systems and across dense webs of other texts.

Multimodality

Multimodality is a way of making sense of texts through linguistic, aural, gestural, visual, and spatial modes (e.g., Kress, 2009). Technically speaking, multimodality is an attribute not of a text but of the reading process itself. For simplicity's sake, though, I refer to a text as *multimodal* if it calls for a multimodal reading. There's an argument to be made that all texts are, in one way or another, multimodal in this sense. After all, even print texts have visual features and layouts that can be read and interpreted. But, to whatever extent multimodality is a spectrum, the pop culture texts we encounter in digital environments are, shall we say, *very* multimodal.

Multimodality decenters language as the primary mode through which texts convey meaning, elevating other modes for analysis and drawing our attention to the way modes work together as an ensemble (Jewitt, 2013, p. 150). For example, if we're watching a TV show, we're attending to words spoken and closed-captioned; we're observing human actions, as they're embodied by actors and framed by directors and camera operators; we're taking in the visual and auditory elements of the setting; and we're picking up on the mood a music cue creates, as well as the actors' tone of voice. There's no avoiding the multimodality of the text.

We read such texts multimodally whether we realize that's what we're doing or not. But we can't be *strategic* in our reading unless we bring self-awareness to the affair. Consciously applying strategy to our reading helps us not only squeeze more meaning out of the text but also read even more actively and critically. Strategic engagement, in other words, is valuable in and of itself and as a way of supporting the other two dimensions of pop culture literacy.

I've found two concepts from scholarship on multimodality especially relevant to our discussion of pop culture literacies: modal affordances (Kress, 1993) and paths through a text (Serafini, 2012, 2015).

Kress (1993) defines **modal affordance** as "what is possible to express and represent easily with a mode" (p. 172). In other words, every mode is uniquely suited to express and represent particular kinds of meanings and messages. One very simple (simplistic) way to think about this is that some modes are governed by the logic of time and others by the logic of space. Spoken language, for example, unfolds over time through linguistic and aural modes. As such, it is uniquely suited to express messages that require information and ideas to be presented in a particular order. Diagrams, on the other hand, make meaning through visual and spatial modes. Diagrams present every element all at once, and so their meanings and messages emerge through the spatial arrangement of visual elements. Diagrams, then, are uniquely suited to convey messages that require understanding of the relationships between parts of a whole.

But, as Hull and Nelson (2005) point out, "A multimodal text can create a different system of signification, one that transcends the collective contribution of its constituent parts" (p. 225). When we examine the modal affordances of a text, then, it's wise to think of the modes as part of an ensemble, rather than in isolation. Take your average TikTok dance challenge. The mise-en-scene, style of dance, and style of dress do not simply supplement, support, or elaborate the song's lyrics. The TikTok's meaning—not to mention its appeal—pivots on the way these modes are coordinated. Modes can elaborate, extend, enhance, or contradict each other. And, as I'll discuss in the next section, they can work together to situate the text within discursive networks of other texts. It's up to us, as strategic readers of pop culture texts, to attend to both the affordances of individual modes and the way those affordances interact with each other.

Today, a mode's affordances are shaped by the devices and technologies we use to engage with texts. Incorporating an image into a written text might be thought of as an attention-grabbing move, assuming an attractive image is more enticing than a big block of words. But today's digital environment is so overwhelmingly visual that an image, just by virtue of being an image, no longer grabs attention. What's one image in an undifferentiated stream of other images?

Let's take the spoken language of a podcast episode. As I described above, spoken language is thought to be governed by the logic of time. The aural and linguistic modes demand our attention over a period of time so that information and ideas can be presented in the intended order. But, today, we put podcasts in our ears and move about our day—running errands, traveling, cooking, cleaning, perhaps falling asleep. A podcast episode can take on an ambient quality, and its meaning and appeal can be just as much about the comfort of a familiar voice in your ear as about the sequential presentation of ideas and information. Podcasts don't demand our attention over time as the radio dramas of yore might have, even though they operate in the same modes.

What a given mode offers is shaped by the way we actually engage with that mode in everyday life. It can never be pinned down once and for all. When we strategically read a pop culture text, we must give some thought to how the modes contribute to and shape the meaning-making process.

To read and make meaning of a pop culture text, or any text, we draw on the text's modes, yes, but we also draw on the experiences, knowledge, and interests we bring to the text. When we read a traditional written text, we decode the words as they are presented across the page. We are, in many ways, at the mercy of the author who selected those words and put them there for us to decode. But because pop culture texts incorporate modes that are seldom, as an ensemble, ruled by time, there is no preset reading path. When we read multimodally, then, we make our own **path through the text** (Serafini, 2012, 2015).

On a practical level, this means that, as readers, we are free to attend to, or ignore, any of the objects or elements in our visual or aural field. The text may be composed to lead us in certain directions, but, ultimately, we as readers choose our own path. Extending the metaphor, Serafini uses the term *navigation* to describe the multimodal reading process: "Navigating multi-modal texts requires readers to decode the written text, and additionally navigate the compositions and structures of design elements and visual images" (p. 28).

Why might two different readers walk away from the same pop culture text with two different interpretations? They navigated the texts differently; they took different paths. Their experiences, knowledge, and interests directed their gaze and attention. The costuming choice that's striking and salient to one reader goes unnoticed by a second reader. And even when readers attend to the same element, that element evokes different feelings, connects to different bodies of knowledge, and is interpreted through the framework of different experiences. These differences, in turn, propel our two readers in divergent directions still.

Of course, what further complicates the paths we take through texts is, again, the fragmentation of our attention across multiple devices. Our unique interpretive paths aren't contained within individual texts. They wind through, across, between, and beyond texts. The setting and context of our reading experience—couch, class, car, subway, waiting room, park bench, bed—shape our paths as much as anything else.

Intertextuality

The meaning of a pop culture text isn't singular, definite, or static. A strategic reader of pop culture texts, therefore, must stay active and attentive in their search for it. In the previous section,

I argued that pop culture texts produce meanings through their ensembles of modes. But meaning, in my view, is more slippery than that suggests. The strategic reader must also account for texts' intertextuality: that their meanings are produced through their connections to other texts. Texts, of course, have always been intertextual in the sense that they've been embedded in genres, movements, time periods, and discursive networks. But today's pop culture texts are, shall we say, *very* intertextual. Here, I'll offer descriptions of three ways in which pop culture texts operate intertextually: referentiality, transmediation, and fragmentation.

A distinctive feature of today's pop culture texts is that they refer to other texts—whether explicitly to individual texts or implicitly to groups of texts. I think of **explicit referentiality** as *allusion*, in the traditional literary sense. To get the humor of the *Saturday Night Live* sketch about a meme, for example, one would have to have seen the meme. In other cases, explicit referentiality is more about importing the mood—or vibe—of the referred-to text. For example, on TikTok, a pop song imbues an otherwise indecipherable video with a mood, a meaning, even a whole narrative. The text can refer to the source text through simple inclusion, through allusion, or through imitation, but the key feature of this category of intertextuality is that one text refers to another text.

More common on social media is a kind of **implicit referentiality** not to individual texts but to whole networks or genres of other texts. Memes can feel silly and unapologetically meaningless (Katz & Shifman, 2017), and they do pick up a lot of randomness as they circulate online and off (Danesi, 2019). Meme culture is all about the remix: texts are "endlessly edited, combined, and manipulated into new creative blends (Katz & Shifman, 2017). Content itself can be remixed, as when a still image or gif is recontextualized through captioning. These images include commercial properties like Baby Yoda, discussed in Chapter 1, but also everyday photos that have become all too familiar to anyone even passingly online: a child grinning mercilessly at the camera before a burning house or a girlfriend looking on with disgust as her boyfriend checks out another woman. Images are pulled from their original contexts and re-appropriated to articulate the user's specific moods, reactions, or perspectives. When memes reuse the same images, or even formats, they implicitly refer to all the other memes that do so. This is also true of other kinds of online content, like the viral dance challenges discussed in Chapter 1 and the fashion influencer genre discussed in Chapter 2.

Fredric Jameson helped us theorize these kinds of referentiality long before the memeification of culture. In *Postmodernism, or the Cultural Logic of Late Capitalism,* Jameson (1991) argued that, in the era of late capitalism and mass culture, artists had abandoned the pursuit of meaning, opting instead for a "depthless imitation" he called *pastiche*. Jameson distinguished pastiche from parody. A work is pastiche when the artist's repetition of ideas and images—think Andy Warhol—does not add any meaning to the original. A work is parody when it does. We can apply the parody/pastiche distinction to today's online content. Individual users might creatively remix, deconstruct, or poke fun at familiar meme content and structure (parody), or they might simply create a substantially similar copy, keeping the hamster wheel of content going. Some have argued that, in meme culture, the sender and recipient are interchangeable, and, therefore, meaning isn't in the content itself but in the act of transmission of content. Or as Marshall McLuhan (1964) famously put it long, long ago: the medium is the message.

Another way pop culture texts operate intertextually is through **transmediation**. *Transmediation* refers to the way a single narrative is told across different media, creating a coherent storyworld (Jenkins, 2006). For example, the narrative of *Star Wars* has been told across films, TV shows, merchandise, books, and video games. Transmediation includes both the content and properties created commercially (films, TV shows, trailers, soundtracks) and those created by audiences (reviews, reactions, commentary, fanfiction). Jenkins described how transmediation makes consumers into "hunters and gatherers, chasing down bits of the story across media channels" (p. 20). *Reading* the narrative is about engaging—even immersing oneself—in the narrative world. Gray (2010) describes the texts associated with a main commercial text as *paratexts*. He writes:

> We are all part-time residents of the highly populated cities of Time Warner, DirecTV, AMC, Sky, Comcast, ABC, Odeon, and so forth, yet not all of these cities' architecture is televisual or cinematic by nature. Rather, these cities are also made up of all manner of ads, previews, trailers, interviews with creative personnel, Internet discussion, entertainment news, reviews, merchandising, guerilla marketing campaigns, fan creations, posters, games, DVDs, CDs, and spinoffs. (p. 1)

Paratexts are resources we use to interpret and discuss the narrative worlds we inhabit. A distinctive feature of paratexts, according to Gray, is that we're so inundated with them that by the time we listen to or watch the thing itself—the album, the show, the film—we've already begun to make meaning of it.

To my mind, there's one more form of intertextuality that can't *not* be mentioned. It's the kind of accidental, fragmented intertextuality created by "staring at the big screen while scrolling through [our] little screen" (Cai, 2020). I seldom find myself engaging with one text at a time but, instead, cast about in an open torrent of texts. And the texts in this torrent take on some relationship to each other by sheer accident of proximity. This sort of intertextuality feels like the logical extension of Jameson's (1991) *pastiche* in the sense that it can be thought of as meaningless and depthless. It's unauthored intertextuality.

Or, if it is authored, it's algorithmically authored. Algorithms suck up data about us, send it through a series of equations, and generate a result supposedly suited to our interests and needs. On one hand, algorithmic culture produces the sort of implicit referentiality I described. As cultural critic Kyle Chayka (2024) put it, the culture algorithms create "is ultimately homogenous, marked by a pervasive sense of sameness even when its artifacts aren't literally the same. It perpetuates itself to the point of boredom" (p. 6).

On the other hand, our engagement with multiple texts at once can produce intertextual meanings that are spontaneous and strange. The screenwriter and director Aaron Sorkin has said that an artist's job is to captivate you for however long they've asked for your attention (Calvario, 2016). With apologies to Mr. Sorkin, of whom I'm a reluctant fan, last night, I watched "Hartsfield's Landing," a Season 3 episode of his early aughts show *The West Wing*, while watching TikToks about how selvedge denim is made. There's choice in that intertextuality, but there's also a good deal of chance. These texts don't refer to each other, or even relate to each other, but to be a strategic reader of pop culture, I have to be aware of how I'm directing my attention across texts—and why.

Snapshots: Strategic Engagement in Everyday Life

Dark Academia

In 2014, K-hole, a trend forecasting collective, added a new term to the fashion lexicon to describe a nothing-special approach to dressing: *normcore*. Normcore was t-shirts, jeans, and sneakers. Normcore was being cool by dressing normal. As Fiona Duncan (2014) pointed out in *New York Magazine*, walking through SoHo in Manhattan, one "could no longer tell if my fellow . . . pedestrians were art kids or middle-aged, middle-American tourists."

The coining of the term, no doubt, extended the trend's life. But, more importantly, its introduction of the suffix *-core* made it suddenly easy to articulate a whole host of other microtrends in the decade to come. Fashion and lifestyle influencers found the suffix particularly useful during the COVID-19 pandemic, when they were desperate to deliver fresh content to a captive online audience with money to burn (Kaur, 2023). *Cottagecore*—prairie dresses, cozy cardigans, shabby-chic interiors, frolicking among wildflowers—was coined in 2018 but spiked in popularity in the early days of the pandemic, when, to people stuck at home, frolicking was both an enticing and COVID-safe activity.

Since then, *balletcore, goblincore, Barbiecore, kidcore, angelcore, royalcore, cowboycore*, among countless others (truly, how high can you count?) have taken hold, if only briefly and in small pockets of the internet. The *-core* suffix opened up a realm of possibility for influencers, content creators, and everyday people. Suddenly, one could conjure a microtrend into existence simply by naming it.

Tomato girl summer, its name modeled after Megan Thee Stallion's song "Hot Girl Summer" (2019), was "inspired by the Mediterranean coast or anywhere where tomato-based dishes are popular. Think Amalfi Gardens, Santorini beaches, and Barcelona streets" (Momenian, 2023). The tomato girl wears breezy cotton or linen dresses in white, red, and tan; puffy sleeves and ruffled skirts; beachy waves and a flick of black eyeliner at night. But, importantly, it's not just what the tomato girl wears. It's what she does. She reads "romance novels at cafés, [lounges] at the beach, and [watches] the sunset from their backyard garden."

The *-core* fashion trends of the late 2010s and early 2020s have given way to whole lifestyle subcultures like *tomato girl summer* and, the subject of this section, *dark academia*. The digital texts that reflect and sustain the subculture on social media—mood boards, flat lay photos and photo collages, lifestyle montages— are, as you might imagine, multimodal and intertextual. Strategic readers of these texts, then, must rise to the occasion they present and read them multimodally and intertextually.

Dark academia has proven to be an especially durable lifestyle subculture. Theater student Sydney Decker runs @myfairesttreasure, a popular dark academia Instagram account. The mood boards she posts combine clothes (plaid, tweed, turtlenecks, sweater vests, loafers); hobbies ("write a letter to your future lover, your past self, or no one in particular & place the letter into an envelope sealed with wax" and "press flowers into journals only written in black ink"); favorite films (*Dead Poets Society* [1989] and *Kill Your Darlings* [2013]); and book recommendations (*Wuthering Heights* [1847], *The Picture of Dorian Gray* [1890–1891], and several novels by the most cherished writer among dark academes: Donna Tartt).

The dark academia hashtag on TikTok surfaces lifestyle montages that reflect and expand Decker's dark academia aesthetic. We see the artifacts of the dark academe's favorite pastimes: mugs, typewriters, fountain pens, candles, record players, leather-bound books, and pages torn from said books. The mise-en-scene typically features such objects arranged artfully in a teen's bedroom and, more often than you'd think, walls covered in torn-out pages. When we're not in a teen's bedroom, we're in the quad of what looks to be an elite private school or college campus: stately oak trees, stone and brick buildings covered in ivy. We see, too, the creator interacting with these objects in these settings: typing on the typewriter, sipping tea, peering up from behind a leather-bound book, tousling one's close crop of waves so they fall just so over their dark-rimmed glasses. Many of these montages are scored by the "dark academia check" sound on TikTok, which features jazz singer Anita O'Day's "Harlem on Parade" (1941). Occasionally, the creator uses video effects that mimic celluloid film: film grain, blips, and sepia tones. Most montages are captioned simply, underlining the activity or detail the viewer is meant to connect to dark academia.

One of the major tenets of the strategic engagement framework is that modes don't work in isolation. They work, instead, as ensembles, elaborating and enhancing each other. This feature of multimodal texts is what allows a microtrend—a relatively small set of sartorial details that cohere around an aesthetic—to blossom into a full-on lifestyle subculture. Once an aesthetic like dark academia has been named and hashtagged, it begins to spiral outward, widening as it pulls more and more items, activities, and visual details into its orbit. While the visual and linguistic modes of captioned mood boards and flat lay photos effectively convey what a dark academe might wear, the visual, linguistic, spatial, gestural, and aural modes of video montages go further. They can convey what the person wearing those items might be thinking, feeling, doing, and buying. And the multimodality of these montages is persuasive. When all the modes are firing at once, even seemingly off-topic details can be pulled into the dark academia vortex. If a person with dark-rimmed glasses and a sweater vest has a diagram of a human skeleton or a music box in their room, suddenly diagrams of human skeletons and music boxes feel very *dark academia*.

The strategic engagement framework also invites us to read these texts intertextually. Dark academia images and videos are explicitly referential, and understanding the references is a prerequisite for interpretation. The books referenced typically fall into one of two categories: canonical 19th-century British literature (especially anything by the Brontë sisters) or the work of the Beats (especially Allen Ginsberg). The latter category is what draws dark academia to the film *Kill Your Darlings*, a biographical film about Allen Ginsberg and the beat poets in their college days. And "Harlem on Parade"? The song used in TikTok's "dark academia check" sound clip is on the *Kill Your Darlings* soundtrack. In this case, referentiality is less a line that connects a text to an external referent and more a web of references that enable meaning-making.

Jake and Ant Fight Every Single Boss

Over the past two decades, as video games have become more accessible, portable, and social, the video game industry has, by all imaginable metrics, boomed (Grand View Research, 2023). I'll begin with a primer on video games for the uninitiated. Video games can be subdivided into overlapping categories, based on the gameplay experience: puzzle, first-person shooter, battle royale, sports, action-adventure, sandbox, role-playing—among many, many others. The most salient factor that distinguishes one game from another is the degree of constraint it puts on the player. On one end of the spectrum, we have linear games, which curate the gameplay experience by presenting a series of tasks or challenges the player must complete in a preset order. New levels are unlocked upon completion of a task, and the game definitively ends at a predetermined point. Games like *God of War* (Santa Monica Studio et al., 2005) and *The Last of Us* (Naughty Dog, 2013) belong to this category.

On the other end of the spectrum are open-world games. In these games, a player can approach objectives freely, roaming the game world with a high degree of autonomy. There are relatively few constraints on the gameplay. The most "open" of these games are sandbox games like *Minecraft* (Mojang Studios, 2011), in which the player has the highest degree of control, making choices about where to go, what to do, and what to create within the game world. These games do not predetermine the player's objectives but provide creative tools the player can use as they see fit.

This spectrum is, of course, crosscut by other aspects of the gameplay experience, and games don't necessarily cluster around one end of the spectrum or the other. Some open-world games have an ending or multiple possible endings determined, in part, by the player's choices. Others are endless. Some games, like *Fortnite* (Epic Games, 2017) can be played in multiple modes. Others, like *Genshin Impact* (MiHoYo, 2020) have both linear and open elements: the player is free to roam the world as they please, but the narrative of the game unfolds in a series of "acts." *Omori* (Omocat, 2020) also has both linear and open elements: the game sets the narrative, but the player has the option to explore the world and go on side quests that are not strictly constrained by this narrative.

Video games are, of course, multimodal texts. All five of the major modes are activated in the meaning-making process: visual, spatial, aural, linguistic, and gestural. Gameplay, however, also involves what has been called the mechanic mode (Arendall, 2023). The mechanic mode refers to the design of the game. Meaning is produced through the player's in-game actions and the consequences they trigger and, in linear games, through preset sequences of tasks and rewards. This sort of modality is connected to what Bogost (2010) called the procedural rhetoric of a video game. To Bogost, video games enable meaning-making by immersing the player in a simulated world where the governing procedures of that world—the way in which actions and consequences interlock—are under the control of the game's author. Bogost emphasized that it's not the narrative content of a video game that holds the rhetorical power to change attitudes and beliefs, but the in-game procedures that are coordinated through code.

It's easy to see how gamers strategically engage in playing video games. Players must actively decide how to participate in the storytelling of the game, given the level of autonomy the game confers. They simultaneously decode meaning as they read the visual, spatial, aural, gestural, and mechanic elements of the game world and encode meaning as they decide how to act.

In the past, game companies expected that their games would be played and enjoyed privately. Today, however, gamers enjoy not only playing games but also watching others play. Video game streamers broadcast their gameplay with live commentary. Sometimes, streamers explain their decision-making as they play, but more often they simply play and react to the game as the consequences of their in-game actions unfold. Viewers can comment and react to the gameplay (or anything else they please) in a chat window. The streamer can see and respond to these messages in real time.

Everyday gamers live-stream to their friends, interacting and bonding with them as they would participating in any other shared activity (Cabeza-Ramírez et al., 2021). But, as we've seen in other industries, in gaming, there's a professional class of video game streamers who've amassed large followings and receive sponsorships for their content. The live-streaming platform Twitch helped cultivate the popularity of both professional streamers themselves and the practice of watching others' gameplay in general. But streamers grow their audiences by cross-posting edited highlight videos of their streams to other platforms, like YouTube and TikTok.

The practice of live-streaming gameplay is not as simple, or simplistic, as it may sound. To draw an audience, streamers must be especially entertaining, especially skilled as gamers, or both. Streaming requires a high degree of strategy and even creativity, executed extemporaneously and highlighted in the editing process. Viewers see three elements in the frame of a highlight video: the gameplay, the streamer's video feed, and the chat. The streamer controls aspects of all three elements in the moment of gameplay and then can manipulate them in the process of editing the video. How do these three elements produce meaning? In the gameplay frame, the streamer makes choices about where their in-game character will go, how they'll move, and how they'll approach tasks. They can also move the in-game camera however they'd like, highlighting different aspects of the game world.

Their inlaid video feed showcases their physical movements, use of the controller, and facial expressions. The streamer's commentary is key to their popularity. Through this commentary, they develop a distinctive persona and establish the nature and tone of the discourse. The streamer might be silly, informative, confessional, disciplined, feisty, and so on. In the live feed, they make choices about the background of their video feed, and, when they edit the highlight video, they can adjust the size and position of the inset. The final element, the chat, is often presented as a scrolling text that runs along one side of the frame. This allows viewers to see how people reacted to the stream when it was live. The highlight videos are edited for maximum entertainment value, showcasing the streamer's distinctive personality and style of gameplay.

I examined one highlight video posted by popular streaming duo Jake Tuonto and Antony Chen (Chen, 2022), friends, former roommates, and professional streamers. If I'd needed convincing that pop culture engagement is and must be strategic, my experience with this particular pop culture text would have done the job. As an outsider to the genre, I struggled to make sense of the splatter of semiosis I was witnessing on the screen. In other words, I had no strategy. The video's commenters, in contrast, did.

The highlight video contains the three elements I described: the gameplay, the video feed, and the chat. These elements are in constant motion. The scrolling chat appears along the left side of the frame in the moments leading up to gameplay, but mostly disappears thereafter. The content of the chat is an enthusiastic jumble of emojis, all-caps greetings, and more than a few references to chicken nuggets (your guess is as good as mine). Antony's video feed is most often inlaid in the corner of the gameplay, but there are also cutaway shots of his feed, as well as Jake's. The duo acts and interacts in the real world, as well as in the game world. We see this when, for example, Antony becomes exasperated when Jake leaves to go to the restroom for an extended period, leaving him vulnerable in the game world. Their interactions feel lived-in, authentic—a quality often noted by their fans in the comments section.

The editing of the video is deliberately heavy-handed and lo-fi: voice distortions, color filters, stock audio effects, music cues, jerky zoom-ins, jiggly pop-ups of game graphics, and melodramatic subtitles work together to supercharge the comedy and the (comedic) drama of both the real-world and game-world interactions. At several points, Antony's and Jake's faces are very crudely superimposed on the faces of characters in what appear to be film stills and clips.

Antony and Jake are playing *Genshin Impact* (MiHoYo, 2020), an open-world role-playing game that takes place in the fantasy world of Teyvat. There are seven nations of Teyvat, and each act of the game takes place in a different nation. Players select characters who have unique abilities to solve puzzles and battle enemies. Bosses are scattered throughout Teyvat, and defeating them allows players to acquire new resources.

Antony lays out the gameplay challenge at the beginning of the video: "My challenge at least for today is to defeat every single boss in the game. We are going to be co-oping this as a duo, each having one character. And every time I die, I will be 10-pulling." *Co-oping* means playing the game collaboratively, and *10-pulling* refers to a particularly risky method of gathering resources for combat. When Jake joins, he claims that he's doing a different challenge that Antony doesn't know about. He teases the conflict their differing objectives will produce, but he ultimately doesn't reveal what it is.

When it comes to video games, strategic engagement isn't just reserved for gameplay. We can see strategic engagement in the viewing of gameplay, as well. In the comments section, viewers actively, strategically, and joyfully make meaning of what they're watching. They interpret the video multimodally and intertextually. And their interpretive gaze is sweeping. They evaluate the game itself ("woah they added a new scream sound for this boss, nice job hoyoverse"); the gameplay ("I have two mains for two Abyss teams but I also use them together in the overworld: Qiqi and Thoma"); the video editing ("Respect to the editor not only for the edits but also because the original fight with raiden lasted longer than this entire video"); and the ever-unfolding story of Antony's and Jake's friendship ("when ant said he has a presentation to do and jake immediately switched to the jade cutter to speed things up? a real one" and "it's just hilarious to me how jake knew and even narrated that when ant put down his earphones, it means he didn't get what he wanted and he's leaving the room, he knows him so well"). Even if some of the meaning was lost on me, I did spend enough time with Antony, Jake, and their fans to appreciate their strategic engagement, and to be, I admit, charmed by the playful, enthusiastic, warm community they'd created with each other.

Strategic Engagement in the Classroom

Strategic Engagement Up Close

We'd missed Group the Friday before Memorial Day for a pep rally, so we decided to convene on a Tuesday over lunch in their ELA classroom. Their teacher took his own lunch elsewhere to accommodate us. On our agenda were scenes from the film *Step Up Revolution* (Feig et al., 2012). But with time wasted on a close read of the food on offer in the cafeteria and a swapping of lunch trays among the girls, we only got to see one. Everyone was there and, eventually, focused on the text at hand, but the conversation felt both looser and more subdued than usual. Salty language was kept to a minimum (perhaps the implicit strictures of meeting during the school day in a "real" classroom), and comments that started with gusto seemed to peter out after a few seconds.

We watched a handful of scenes from *Step Up Revolution* before landing on the one the group was most eager to discuss. In the scene, the protagonist Emily, wearing a flouncy silver minidress and glittering volto mask, leads a flash-mob-style dance in a restaurant. The male dancers wear dark suits, and the other female dancers wear dark dresses that otherwise match hers. The lighter color of her dress, as well as the choreography and filmwork, marks her as the star of the troupe.

The group interpreted the scene through spatial, visual, and gestural modes (the filmwork, costuming, and choreographed dance, respectively). While everyone but Danielle had already seen the film—as well as other properties in the *Step Up* cinematic universe—our discussion didn't much concern the textual narrative. Instead, the group, taking an endostory stance, read Emily's motivations and goals through her style of dress and dance.

Kayla opened the discussion seeking clarity on the distinction between the words *sexist* and *sexy*. Danielle, with notes of exasperation in her voice, clarified the distinction for her. *Sexy* turned out to be the word she was looking for to describe Emily's style of dance. Then, Audrey offered a complicated evaluation of Emily's dress:

> She was opening [her legs] all over. Like, you can see anything, underwear . . . Yeah, she was prepared for the dance, so she had gymnastics shorts things under. But, like, still. You wouldn't just get up and start walking on a table where someone was eating. She had a short dress on. I wouldn't really say it was a club dress, but it was really short.

Audrey began with reproval ("you can see anything, underwear") and then veered toward concession ("she had gymnastics shorts things under") and back again ("You wouldn't just get up and start walking on the table"). She repeated this basic structure in her final assessment: *short dress, but not a club dress, but still really short.*

Brianna then opened the discussion wider: "I think the video made the girl look outstanding. It made her seem like she was a good dancer because she did a twirl thingy and she landed. It was made for her to stand out." The antecedent of "it" in Brianna's statement isn't entirely clear, and, by extension, it's not clear if she's taking an endostory or exostory stance. Her comment begins with a reference to the video, so she might be referring to the director's framing of the shots. But she goes on to describe the choreography (the "twirl thingy").

Nevertheless, her interpretation—that Emily is *outstanding*, that she *stands out*—set into motion a meandering exchange of supporting evidence. Brianna first went on to comment that the men are "too stiff" in their dance style and then demonstrated how the women dance in contrast, making serpentine movements with her arms.

Audrey: [The men] dance with, like—
Jaylee:—with clothes
Audrey: Yeah, with clothes. And she had this short dress on like I said before. Also because Brianna said—They're not like, I mean—She's, like, curvy? I don't know if that's the right word. She's able to move her hips and stuff. And if there are creeps, they're like "Yeah!" They'll just take her. That's creepy.

I interjected to confirm that Audrey meant that the men in the audience (diegetically speaking) were the ones who are creepy in leering at her, and then turned our attention back to the costuming differences between men and women in the scene.

Kayla: [The women's clothes] are more open. She knows how to express her body.
Audrey: Maybe she's expressing her feelings with her dance.

What stands out to me about this exchange is the way the group negotiated meaning using a combination of visual and gestural modes. Brianna and Audrey emphasized and pulled the conversation back to the style of dance, whereas Jaylee and Kayla focused on the style of dress. I don't hear disagreement or contradiction in their exchange. They each took an individual path through the text during viewing—it's impossible to know where that path took them. But, in conversation, they co-constructed a path back through the text. This conversational path wound back and forth between the visual and the gestural, and the meanings they arrived at together perfectly illustrate the idea that multimodal ensembles are more than the sum of their parts. When it comes to interpreting what this character is doing and why, the dance and the dress are inextricable. The style of dress amplifies the effect of the dance, and the style of dance amplifies the effect of the dress. How could she "express her body" without both?

The group arrived at their ultimate appraisal of the clip through an intertextual reading. Jasmine, taking an exostory stance and telling a probable story, concluded that an unnamed *they* "made her dance like that because people normally see women like that because normally women are strippers or something."

"And also music videos these days?" Kaylee interjected. "Music videos would be mostly about girls that [are] like half naked, barely any clothes on."

Danielle offered the final word: "I think her dancing . . . was meant for her to be seen as, I guess, sexy even though the audience for the movies can range, can be little kids."

Here, Jasmine, Kaylee, and Danielle are emphasizing the implicit referentiality of the dancing. Interestingly, when I read the clip multimodally, I don't see much resemblance to the kind of dancing in, say, A Boogie's "Timeless" music video (which the group wouldn't watch until the following week). But perhaps that's because I took a different path through the text. The girls' focus was trained on the costuming and the choreography, whereas I had directed my attention to the arrangement of the dancers in the frame and the overall effect of the staging, camerawork, and editing.

Teaching Possibilities

In these discussions, the girls and I took distinctive paths through the text, drew on the ensembles of modes the texts deploy, and synthesized knowledge of other texts to make sense of the text before us. These are the seeds of strategic engagement. We can cultivate strategic engagement by bringing purpose, awareness, and choice to our reading: a specific purpose for engaging with the text, awareness of oneself as a reader and awareness of the text, and intentional choice in how to proceed.

The questions in Table 3.1 are meant to help students develop awareness, purpose, and choice. They can apply to any text students read, in or out of school, on any device or platform. They can be used for private reflection or group discussion.

TABLE 3.1 Supporting strategic interpretation, response, and composition in the classroom.

Interpretation

Purpose: What is my purpose for engaging with this text?

Awareness of Text:

♦ What modes—linguistic, aural, gestural, visual, spatial, mechanic—does the text use?

♦ How do these modes work together and/or against each other to make ideas and information available to the reader?

♦ What does the text assume I know about other texts?

♦ What other texts is this text calling to mind, invoking, or directly referencing?

♦ How does this text connect to those other texts: content, structure, style?

♦ Am I the audience the creator of this text had in mind?

♦ How does this text direct me to think or feel differently about myself, about the world, or about the subject at hand?

Awareness of Self:

♦ What path am I taking through this text?

♦ How does the device, platform, or context in which I'm engaging with this text affect my reading?

♦ What knowledge of other texts am I bringing to my interpretation?

♦ What knowledge am I lacking?

Choice:

♦ What is there to notice in this text, beyond what I instinctively and immediately noticed?

♦ What other possible paths could I take or might others take through the text?

♦ Why am I choosing my path over these others?

♦ Does my path suit my purpose?

♦ How am I working with or against the design of the device, platform, or context in which I'm engaging with the text?

Response and Composition

Purpose:

♦ How do I want to contribute to or interact with the community in which this text was produced and circulated?

♦ What could be my purpose in crafting and sharing a response to this text?

Awareness of Self:

♦ How do I currently interact with and/or contribute to the community in which this text was produced and circulated?

♦ How do others interact and contribute?

♦ How do I want others to engage with what I say or compose?

Choice:

♦ What genre of response or composition would suit my purpose?

♦ What aspects or elements of the original text do I want to incorporate or respond to in my own response or composition?

♦ What do I have to say?

Exercises for Teachers
Interpretation Exercises

The questions above are a good starting point as you prepare to support students in becoming more strategic in their engagement with pop culture texts. As always, you can deepen your own reflections by tapping into how pop culture affects you.

♦ In what situations do you feel your strategic mind turn on?

♦ When you're engaging strategically, what works for you, and what doesn't?

♦ What makes strategic engagement challenging?

♦ Consider the multimodal texts you enjoy the most. What kinds of meaning do those texts' modes make possible?

♦ Are there particular moments when you're in the mood for a particular kind of text: a song vs. a podcast, for example, or a TV show vs. a film? What do you think affects those moods? How do these different kinds of texts affect you differently?

♦ When you're engaging with a multimodal text, try out different paths through the texts and reflect on how those different paths help you arrive at different interpretations.

♦ On social media, notice how you scroll, when you pause, how one post relates to another in your sense-making. Notice moments of disjuncture and tension in the juxtaposition of different kinds of texts and meanings. When do you look at comments and when do you not? Why do you or do you not do that?

Response Exercise

Choose a pop culture text that has been on your mind and respond to it either online or in in-person discussion with someone. Whether online or in-person, track the strategies you and others use to make meaning. What modes do you and others use to interpret the text? What paths did you take through the text, and what paths back through the text do you and others take in conversation? What other texts do you and others bring up to make sense of the primary text?

Composition Exercise

Select a pop culture text that's been on your mind and compose content in response to it. This might be a reaction video, a recap, a meme (that follows an existing meme format or not), a gif, or anything else you might imagine. Make strategic choices about which aspects of the original text you pull into your composition and the modes you use to express your ideas. Share it with someone!

Final Note: Me Against the Machine

To understand what it means for young people to be active, critical, and strategic consumers of pop culture, we must start by understanding what it means for us. Recently, I was feeling disillusioned by my own social media engagements—and pessimistic about the possibility of being strategic. My feeds had been overrun by AI-generated slop and misdirected ads (if my algorithm were to be believed, I was somehow both menopausal and pregnant; I was neither).

Resolving to practice what I preach, I tried to bring some strategy to my social media engagement. I vowed to really look at each post, each scrap of content, to take it seriously and try to understand it. That required me to slow down, look, think, and feel. I also actively tried to resist the design of the apps. This meant, for example, using the "Following" function on Instagram—a reverse chronological feed of only the accounts one follows—and choosing which accounts' Instagram Stories to look at. The latter took a lot of vigilance and practice. I didn't want Stories to auto-advance to the next account or to an ad, so, as I engaged with each Story, I held my finger on the screen to freeze it. Before releasing it, I glanced at the progress bar to determine how many more Stories were posted in the set. This was my strategy—it was hard.

The experience highlighted the contrast between what I do and don't want to see on social media. It made me appreciate the beauty, range, and depth of the multimodal offerings: the selvedge denim videos, artsy photos of young couples lazing about in the grass in Rome, funny memes about the apocrypha of quicksand, instructional videos on how to get an egg to not stick to a stainless steel pan, protest poems and art I'd likely not encounter otherwise, and, of course, pictures of my friends' babies. I came to love and detest the whole enterprise in equal measure.

The three parts of the pop literacy framework—active engagement, critical engagement, and strategic element—are interconnected. While each element has its own distinct emphasis, it is, in fact, impossible to have any one element without the others. How could one actively engage with pop culture without also having a strategic purpose and method? How could one be a critical reader of pop culture texts without the strategy it takes to understand how they operate multimodally and intertextually? And what good is a strategy, really, that isn't held up by an undercurrent of active and critical engagement?

I didn't fully appreciate these interconnections until I tried out the literacy practices I'm espousing myself. I conclude Part One, then, with a nudge for you to do the same. As you prepare to teach pop culture literacy, do the thing you'll ask young people to do. Find out what makes it hard and what makes it worth it.

References

Arendall, D. E. (2023). *The language of league: Making sense of multimodal meaning in Twitch live streams* (Publication no. 30569716) [Doctoral dissertation; The University of Memphis]. ProQuest Dissertations & Theses Global.

Bogost, I. (2010). *Persuasive games: The expressive power of videogames.* MIT Press.

Cabeza-Ramírez, L. J., Muñoz-Fernández, G. A., & Santos-Roldán, L. (2021). Video game streaming in young people and teenagers: Uptake, user groups, dangers, and opportunities. *Healthcare, 9*(2), 1–16.

Cai. D. (2020, November 22). another day of staring at the big screen while scrolling through my little screen so as to reward myself for staring at the medium screen all week [Post]. X. https://x.com/delia_cai/status/1330597127131684870?lang=en

Calvario, L. (2016, July 27). Aaron Sorkin's AMA: 10 highlights include screenwriting tips & possibility of "Studio 60" season 2. *IndieWire*. www.indiewire.com/news/general-news/aaron-sorkins-ama-10-highlights-ask-me-anything-session-1201710639/

Chayka, K. (2024). *Filterworld: How filters are changing how we see ourselves, and everything else*. Graywolf Press.

Chen, A. [antonychenn] (2022). We fought every single boss in *Genshin Impact* [Video]. YouTube. www.youtube.com/watch?v=lnxFskQk2il

Danesi, M. (2019). Memes and the future of pop culture. *Popular Culture*, *1*(1), 1–81.

Duke, N. K., & Cartwright, K. B. (2021). The science of reading progresses: Communicating advances beyond the simple view of reading. *Reading Research Quarterly, 56*, S25–S44.

Duncan, F. (2014, February 26). Normcore: Fashion for those who realize they're one in 7 billion. *New York Magazine*. www.thecut.com/2014/02/normcore-fashion-trend.html

Epic Games. (2017). *Fortnite* [Video game]. Epic Games.

Feig, E., Gibgot, J., Shankman, A., Wachsberger, P. (Producers) & Speer, S. (Director). (2012). *Step up revolution* [Film]. Lionsgate.

Frankel, D. (Director). (2006). *The Devil wears Prada* [Film]. 20th Century Fox.

Grand View Research. (2023). Global video game market size & outlook, 2023–2030. *Horizon Grand View Research*. www.grandviewresearch.com/horizon/outlook/video-game-market-size/global

Gray, J. (2010). *Show sold separately: Promos, spoilers, and other media paratexts*. NYU Press.

Hull, G. A., & Nelson, M. E. (2005). Locating the semiotic power of multimodality. *Written Communication, 22*(2), 224–261.

Jameson, F. (1991). *Postmodernism, or the cultural logic of late capitalism*. Duke University Press.

Jenkins, H. (2006). *Convergence culture: Where old and new media collide*. NYU Press.

Jewitt, C. (2013). Multimodality and digital technologies in the classroom. In I. de Saint-Georges & J. Weber (Eds.), *Multilingualism and multimodality* (pp. 141–152). Sense Publishers.

Katz, Y., & Shifman, L. (2017). Making sense? The structure and meanings of digital memetic nonsense. *Information, Communication & Society, 20*(6), 825–842.

Kaur, R. (2023, December 5). Project rapid runway: Unraveling the insidious threads of fast fashion. *The [F]law*. https://theflaw.org/articles/project-rapid-runway-unraveling-the-insidious-threads-of-fast-fashion/

Kress, G. (1993). Against arbitrariness: The social production of the sign as a foundational issue in critical discourse analysis. *Discourse and Society, 4*(2), 169–193.

Kress, G. (2009). *Multimodality: A social semiotic approach to contemporary communication*. Routledge.

McLuhan, M. (1964). *Understanding media: The extensions of man*. Routledge.

MiHoYo. (2020). *Genshin impact* [Video game]. HoYoverse; CHN: miHoYo; VNM: Funtap; TWN/HKG/MAC: Nijigen Games.

Mojang Studios. (2011). *Minecraft* [Video game]. Mojang Studios; Xbox Game Studios.

Momenian, D. (2023, July 3). What is tomato girl summer? Tiktok's latest trend is not what it seems. *Teen Vogue*. www.teenvogue.com/story/tiktok-tomato-girl-summer-aesthetic-trend-explained

Naughty Dog. (2013). *The last of us* [Video game]. Sony Computer Entertainment.

Omocat. (2020). *Omori* [Video game]. Omocat.

Santa Monica Studio, Ready at Dawn, & Javaground/SOE-LA[c]. (2005). *God of war* [Video game]. Sony Interactive Entertainment; Sony Pictures Digital.

Serafini, F. (2012). Reading multimodal texts in the 21st century. *Research in the Schools, 19*(1), 26–32.

Serafini, F. (2015). Multimodal literacy: From theories to practices. *Language Arts, 92*(6), 412–423.

Swift, T., & Antonoff, J. (2020). August [Song; recorded by Taylor Swift]. On *Folklore*. Republic.

Swift, T., & Antonoff, J. (2022). You're on your own, kid [Song; recorded by Taylor Swift]. On *Midnights*. Republic.

Wind, E. (2024, February 7). What's behind the Taylor Swift friendship bracelets trend? *The Guardian*. www.theguardian.com/music/2024/feb/07/taylor-swift-eras-tour-australia-friendship-bracelets-inspiration-beads-explained

Part Two

Pop Culture Literacy Lessons

4

The Foundations of Pop Culture Literacy

Introduction to Part Two: Pop Culture Literacy Lessons

Each chapter in the second half of the book presents five lessons that teach adolescents and teens how to engage with pop culture more actively, critically, and strategically. I begin each chapter with a section called "Finding Mentors." In this section, I identify pop culture literacy mentors. These are real people—podcast hosts, a film director, and a memoirist—who engage with pop culture in ways we'd want young people to. I offer these mentors to give you a sense of what we might hope the outcome of our pop culture literacy instruction to be.

After I describe how the mentors engage with pop culture texts, I present the chapter's lessons. The plans for these lessons are detailed, not because I think they must be taught exactly the way they're written, but because I hope to be clear and compelling in presenting what I've envisioned. The specifics of your lessons—as well as their power and charm—will come from you, your students, and the ways you've devised to engage with pop culture in the particular worlds you inhabit.

DOI: 10.4324/9781032667027-7

Finding Mentors: Recap Culture

In the fall of 2016, I developed two interdependent pop culture interests: *Gilmore Girls* (2000–2007), the early aughts TV dramedy, and *Gilmore Guys* (Porter & Adejuyigbe, 2014–2017), the podcast about it. My nighttime routine consisted of watching one episode of the show, semi-ambiently, as I got ready for bed and then falling asleep to the associated podcast episode. My engagement with each text multiplied the pleasure of engaging with the other.

Hosted by comedian Kevin T. Porter and TV writer Demi Adejuyigbe, the podcast followed the friends as they watched every episode of the TV show—Porter as a longtime fan and Adejuyigbe as a newcomer. *Gilmore Guys* was my first rewatch podcast (there are now several in my rotation), and, from early on, I found that the hosts' discussions of the show, and more than occasional digressions into other pop culture topics, gave me new ways of thinking about pop culture literacy. Porter and Adejuyigbe would weave in and out of the narrative of the show, just as pleased to chitchat about the characters' lives as they were to critique the show's production and writing and analyze it as a cultural product of its time. Sometimes, they seemed to do it all in one breath.

The podcast models the kind of pop culture literacy featured in this chapter's lessons. Let's look at an episode in which Porter and Adejuyigbe (2015) discussed the *Gilmore Girls* episode "A House Is Not a Home" (Sherman-Palladino, 2005) with guest Aisha Muharrar. In the episode, the three discussed a pivotal scene: Lorelai Gilmore, reeling from a recent rift with her daughter-slash-best-friend Rory, spontaneously proposes to her boyfriend Luke. This exchange exemplifies the kind of active, self-aware reading that I've come to hope for in my work with young people.

> **Porter:** So *Lorelai* is the one who proposes to *Luke*. I think this is a genius story move, and I 100% disagree with it on a reality level. . . . Of course, Lorelai would do this. Of course, Lorelai would cling onto the one man who's always been there for

her, who's been her confidante, and *blah blah blah blah blah* in a time of emotional turmoil and struggle. This is such a close parallel to what happened in [episode] 422. It's a real echo of it, and not in a way that feels recycled. But is—oh, something terrible is happening with Rory, and something great is happening with Luke.

Muharrar: Poor Rory. I mean, Rory hasn't had an easy go of it since that Dean incident.

Adejuyigbe: Rory is going to end up in jail again, and then Luke is going to find out that Lorelai is pregnant.

Porter: The more horrible the thing is to Rory—

Adejuyigbe: "I have some bad news: Rory passed away." "Hello, I'm from *Publisher's Clearinghouse!*"

Porter: It's a one-for-one. It's an echo of that that doesn't feel like a cheat. It's this story still—the different arcs of Lorelai and Rory. It just seems like a terrible move on Lorelai's part.

The three then drift into discussion of proposal metaphors, eating habits, and doctor's visits before Muharrar returns to Porter's original idea:

Muharrar: Yes, I think—it's not a good thing to do but very much in character. Yes, that's weird timing. It puts Luke in a weird position, but that kind of seems like something Lorelai would do. Were you surprised, Demi?

Adejuyigbe: Here's the thing. I knew it was coming when he started talking, and she was about to say something. This show—maybe it's because we're ten years out of the show, and I feel like the things that are done have also been done by later shows, so I kind of get the language of it. But when she was focusing on him, she's going to say something really big right now. It's the finale, they haven't ended on anything. When it happened, I also went like, they're both making big decisions based on emotion. Both Rory and Lorelai, and I think both of their decisions are maybe the right move. Maybe Rory needs to drop out of college and focus on journalism or whatever her dream is full-time.

But she's making the decision based on a wrong reason. Of course, Lorelai should marry Luke. That's why—that's the end goal of the entire show.

In their interpretations of the scene, both Porter and Adejuyigbe moved into the narrative to comment on the characters' actions ("of course, Lorelai would do this" and "they're both making big decisions based on emotion") and then stood back from, and outside of, the narrative to analyze the show's writing ("This is such a close parallel to what happened in [episode] 422"). Adejuyigbe drew on the multimodality of the text ("But then she was focusing on him, she's going to say something really big right now") and its intertextuality ("I feel like the things that are done have also been done by other shows, so I kind of get the language of it"). I suggest we look to Porter, Adejuyigbe, and Muharrar as pop culture mentors. In this episode, they actively modulated their interpretations of the text and negotiated meaning together.

Podcasts like *Gilmore Guys* are part of *recap culture*, a term used to describe the proliferation of both podcasts about TV shows and regular TV recap columns in news outlets like *The New York Times*, *New York Magazine's* Vulture, and *A.V. Club*. Wendy Syfret (2019), writing for *The Guardian*, explained the virtue of the TV recap:

Much of my appreciation (and understanding) of the complex plot [of a TV show] and its real-world references is supported by the framework of recap articles and podcasts I turn to when the credits roll. They do more than remind me of what happened on a show I watched minutes earlier; they contextualize rivers of information that might have flowed past me.

Recap culture, according to Syfret, both sustains and enhances the viewing experience.

Since its beginnings on the website *Television Without Pity*, the television recap has grown into its own genre of pop culture commentary, blending analysis, critique, and zeal into basic recaps of plot events. The recap genre shows how it might be possible to deliberately switch between endostory and exostory readings, to both get swept away by the story and maintain one's critical footing. It shows how we might negotiate the meaning we make of a text personally as we affiliate, or don't affiliate, with characters. It shows how essential multimodality and intertextuality are in understanding what we watch. And, most importantly, it shows us how we can orient ourselves toward pop culture texts actively and intentionally, with an awareness of our own purposes of engagement.

Lessons on the Foundations of Pop Culture Literacy

The goal of the five lessons in this chapter is to help young people build a foundation of self-awareness and intentionality in their pop culture reading practices. Self-awareness allows us to exercise deliberate and thoughtful control over how we interpret and respond to pop culture texts.

The sequence of lessons begins with an inquiry into how students are already engaging with pop culture texts. Then, in Lessons 2–4, students develop frameworks and terminology that can help them notice the nuances in what they do as readers and, eventually, make more intentional choices about what, why, and how they read pop culture. In the final lesson, students look to the future and develop pop culture reading resolutions.

These lessons are grounded in the broad definition of *text* I offered in the Introduction and put to use in the chapters since. Lesson 1 might be the first time students think of things like TikToks, movies, and songs as texts, and, moreover, texts that belong to the same broad category as the literature, primary and secondary sources, and scientific journal articles they read in school. The lesson asks students to think of all these texts, nonjudgmentally, as *texts* regardless of their provenance and regardless of who's telling them to read them and why. Hopefully, with this framing, students will see that they can, and perhaps already do, bring the same kind of intentionality and strategy to pop culture texts as they do to academic texts.

Lesson 1: Initial Inquiry

The purpose of this first lesson is to foster students' awareness of their own pop culture and academic reading practices. This sort of self-awareness allows us, as readers, to make more intentional choices about what, why, and how we read. At the top of the lesson, we define *text* explicitly as any object created by humans that makes meaning available to others. The hope is that this broad definition will help students recognize the full range of texts they read in and out of school, without judging their relative worthiness. Then, we invite students to investigate the texts they read across a typical week, detecting patterns in the texts themselves and the strategies they use to make sense of them. Students reconstruct a typical weekday and weekend day of reading, teasing out the kinds of texts they read and their purposes for reading them.

The major work of the lesson is to create a preliminary overview of daily reading habits and set an intention to track reading over the week to come.

Opening and Invitation

Open the lesson by defining *text* as we'll use it in these lessons: any object created by humans that makes meaning available to others. Offer a few examples of texts beyond those that students might immediately think of (for example, TikToks, movies, articles of clothing, songs, and sporting events can all be thought of as *texts*).

Invite students to list all the texts—or kinds of texts—they read in a week. Then, have them share their lists with a partner or two, adding to their own lists as their partners spark new ideas. Guide students to work together to create categories for the different kinds of texts they read. For example, students might distinguish between texts they read by choice and those they read because they're made to. They might also distinguish between different media, genres, or platforms.

Finally, in a whole-class setting, have students share some examples of the texts they read and the categories that emerged in their small-group discussions. Guide their attention to the question of *why* we read these texts. Invite students to share their purposes for reading the texts they typically read, affirming and encouraging honest answers about academic texts (*because you made us write a paper about it!*) and online texts (*because I want to turn my mind off*).

Introduction of New Ideas

Make a case for the value of being more self-aware as readers. Emphasize that, when we're self-aware, we're better able to control and modulate the way we read and make more intentional choices that help us pursue goals and purposes that matter to us.

Share a model of how you've represented the different kinds of texts you read in a typical weekday and weekend day. Your model should include what texts you read, roughly when and for how long, and why you read them (Figure 4.1 shows an example of this model). Point out that this is just a preliminary overview of our reading habits and that we'll track our reading over the next week or so to better understand our actual habits.

Major Work of the Lesson

Students independently create their own preliminary overviews of the texts they read on a typical weekday and a typical weekend day. These overviews emphasize *what* they read and *why* they read. The next step is for students to reflect on *how* they read. To invite them into this reflection, ask questions that address different dimensions of the reading experience and have students reflect loosely in writing. For example:

- How do you typically come upon or access the text?
- How do you make sense of what the author or creator intended?
- How do you deepen or extend your understanding of the text?
- What do you find yourself thinking about as you read?
- What do you intentionally try to think about as you read?
- What tips would you give others trying to read this kind of text?

Reading Week

	Weekday	Weekend
Morning	**Text:** *TikToks, IG posts/stories* **Purpose:** *Get caught up with friends and world* **Text:** *News items (NPR and NYT)* **Purpose:** *Know what's happening in the world, decide what I think, what to do* **Text:** *Teachers' unit/lesson plans* **Purpose:** *Give feedback and support teachers with curriculum*	**Text:** *TikToks, IG posts/stories* **Purpose:** *Get caught up with friends and world* **Text:** *On-repeat playlist* **Purpose:** *Daydream, allow mind to wander while I run errands or do chores* **Text:** *TikToks, IG posts/stories* **Purpose:** *No purpose, just a habit while I do other things*
Afternoon	**Text:** *Education research and other academic articles* **Purpose:** *Prepare to lead discussions in class* **Text:** *TikToks, IG posts/stories* **Purpose:** *Give myself a break from work by entertaining myself*	**Text:** *Novel/memoir* **Purpose:** *Connect with other humans, stories, perspectives; be entertained and enriched* **Text:** *Recipe for "project" meal* **Purpose:** *Learn how to make a new/interesting dish*
Evening	**Text:** *TV show episode (new)* **Purpose:** *Connect with other humans, stories, perspectives; be entertained* **Text:** *TV show episodes (rewatch)* **Purpose:** *Feel comfort of familiar stories and characters* **Text:** *Podcasts* **Purpose:** *Put myself to sleep*	**Text:** *Movie in theater* **Purpose:** *Socialize with friends, connect over shared experience* **Text:** *Podcasts* **Purpose:** *Put myself to sleep*

FIGURE 4.1 Model of an overview of a typical reading week.

Closing and Reflection

Students close the lesson by sharing some of their responses to the reflection questions with the class. Document the strategies, processes, and practices students mention either on a chart or digitally. Set students up to track their reading over the next week with a digital or physical tracker.

Remixes

Teach this lesson as a standalone lesson at the beginning of the school year. Students' reconstructions of their reading habits can help you get to know them as readers and as people. It might also help you find opportunities to make connections between the academic texts you teach and the texts students engage with in their personal lives.

Embed ideas from this lesson into other lessons about the importance of reading with purpose. Invite students to generate lists of texts they typically read as a do now or warm-up. This activity helps highlight how our purpose for reading shapes our reading strategies. Clearly defining our purpose for reading and monitoring the extent to which we're fulfilling that purpose are at the heart of active self-regulation, an essential element of successful reading (Duke & Cartwright, 2021).

Lesson 2: Relationships with Characters

This lesson asks students to consider how they relate to the characters in the texts they read. Here, a *character* refers not only to a fictional character in the traditional sense but also to any person—or idea of a person—who operates as a character in a text. For example, a historical figure can be thought of as a *character* in a primary source document. The implied speaker in a meme is a character. In the course of this work, students learn about the concept of *character affiliation*, or a reader's personal identification with a character in a text, and the ways in which that identification can shape their interpretations of a text. In the lesson, students identify the characters with whom they affiliate and reflect on how their affiliations—or lack thereof—affect their reading experiences overall.

The major work of this lesson is to create a character affiliation map. Students will select a character with whom they affiliate and map out their reasons for affiliating with that character and the ways in which the affiliation shapes their reading of the text and the word.

Opening and Invitation

To open the lesson, share a small set of clips or snippets of pop culture texts that feature at least one obvious main character, whether that be a fictional main character in the traditional sense, a person, or an idea of a person, who's featured prominently in the text. Curate this set of examples with care, selecting a range of media, genres, and characters—including some that are likely to be familiar and appealing to students and others that aren't. Consider incorporating the kinds of texts listed below. The examples in parentheses are for illustrative purposes only; they are relevant at the time of my writing, but likely less relevant at the time of your reading.

- A clip—or a compilation of clips—from a popular TV show or film ("Wednesday Addams Being the Ultimate Mood" [Still Watching Netflix, 2022])
- A pop song with a strong narrative element (Sabrina Carpenter's [2024] "Espresso")
- A TikTok or YouTube video that is grounded in a situation, authentic or constructed ("Saying Yes to the Most SPOILED KID in America for 24 Hours" [Matter, 2024])
- A clip of a pivotal moment in sports featuring a known athlete whose performance or choices affect the larger outcome
- A video game streamer's highlight video ("We Fought Every Single Boss in *Genshin Impact*" [Chenn, 2022])
- Any meme that purports to be relatable to teens

Share each text with the class and direct students to rate each character based on how much they relate to them and explain in writing why they do or don't.

Introduction of New Ideas

Introduce the concept of *character affiliation*. Character affiliation happens when we relate to a character, or align ourselves with a character, to such a degree that they come to guide our overall reading experience. Stipulate that a *character*, in this case, might be a fictional character, a real person who's featured prominently in the text, or an idea of a person; connect these different types of characters to the characters featured in the pop culture examples you shared in the opening of the lesson.

Highlight the following points:

- ◆ The characters with whom we affiliate shape our path through the text. We pay special attention to parts of the text that connect to the character
- ◆ When we affiliate with a character, we care about their inner world (their feelings, traits, and motivations), and we tend to root for them and defend their actions
- ◆ When we affiliate with a character, we might find ourselves talking about them like they're a real person we know
- ◆ We might find ourselves experiencing the character's feelings, good and bad, along with the character

To set up the major work of the lesson, share a model of an affiliation map (see example in Figure 4.2). The affiliation map includes the character with whom you affiliate, reflections on why you affiliate with that character, and details about how that affiliation affects both your reading of the text and your reading of the world.

Major Work of the Lesson

Invite students to share and discuss their ratings for the characters from the pop culture examples, focusing on those

Character Affiliation Map

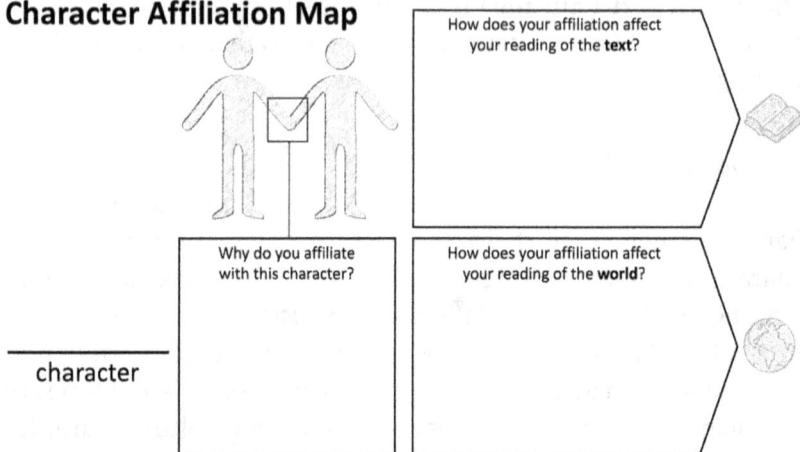

FIGURE 4.2 Character affiliation map graphic organizer.

with whom they affiliate. They might also choose to talk about other characters from other texts with whom they affiliate. Offer students some questions they can use to guide their discussion. For example:

◆ With whom have you affiliated, and why?
◆ How has your affiliation affected what you focus on or what you think about as you engage with the text?
◆ How might the character affect the way you think about yourself, life, or the world outside of the text?

Then, have students independently create an affiliation map for a character of their choice.

Closing and Reflection

Students share parts of their affiliation maps with small groups or the whole class. As students share, guide them to discuss how their reflections might prompt them to think about or approach their pop culture reading differently in the future.

Remixes

Teach this lesson as a standalone lesson in a larger unit about character study in literary fiction. This lesson can launch an inquiry into how writers develop and position characters to elicit feelings of affiliation with readers. Alternatively, teach this lesson as a standalone lesson in a social studies or history unit. This lesson can be used to help students explore the extent to which we, as individuals living at this time and in this place, relate or don't relate to others across time and geographic place. Consider curating the examples you share with students to fit the broader purposes of your discipline and your unit of study.

Embed ideas from this lesson into other lessons. For example, embed the idea of character affiliation into literature lessons about characterization by inviting students to select a character from a novel with whom they affiliate and map out their affiliation. In a social studies or history class, have students create a similar map once they've studied several important historical figures from a particular period or historical event.

Lesson 3: Endostory vs. Exostory

This lesson introduces two reading stances we can take when we read stories: endostory and exostory. The purpose of introducing and naming these two stances is to increase students' awareness of themselves as readers of narrative texts, whether they're academic or pop culture texts. When we take an endostory stance, we derive a lot of pleasure from our reading. We're swept up in the story, and we truly feel what the characters and people in the story feel. In contrast, when we take an exostory stance, we're better able to be critical and analytical about the text as something that was constructed by people who had a specific purpose and wanted to have a specific effect on readers.

The major work of this lesson is to launch a self-inquiry to determine the stances we take when we read different kinds of texts for different purposes in different settings.

Opening and Invitation

Frame the opening activity as an experiment. In small groups, students discuss two texts: first, a shared literary text from a

TABLE 4.1 Sample discussion quotes, categorized as endostory or exostory.

	Endostory	*Exostory*
Literary Texts	The dad is such a frustrating character. He's trying to seem genuine, but, at the end of the day, the fact is that he's the adult in the situation, and he has to take responsibility. But why would [character] lie about such an important thing? The unanswered question for me is: why does she hate her mother so much? She already hated her even when her father was still alive, so it wasn't just about his death.	How do you all think the story would be different, or how would we experience it differently, if the author told us the race of each character? I like how the author gradually drops in more information about [character], which helps us to resonate and empathize with her without judgment. But we're supposed to judge [characters'] choices. Their stories are sort of parallel, but opposite. They make different choices at this key moment which puts them on different paths.
Pop Culture Texts	But [character] was so disloyal! What are you supposed to do as a friend, put yourself first or others? I hear they're getting a divorce, or maybe it was a sham marriage from the beginning. Because you never actually see them interacting anymore. [Character] is the best for hand-to-hand combat. If you want to actually beat that level, you need to play her.	The whole ASMR voice thing is supposed to put you in a trance. It's like you can't scroll away because that voice is just so pleasant. Wait, but she's actually playing both characters. She's just in a dark wig in that scene. So maybe it's saying something about how she has multiple identities or personalities. The whole point of the video, though, is to mock other influencers. She's trying to show that she's different and better than them, but is she really?

recent unit and, second, a short, self-contained narrative pop culture text you've presented to the class. Each discussion lasts three minutes, and group members can discuss whatever they'd like to discuss about the text. One member of the group is a scribe, responsible for noting as many direct quotes as possible from the discussion.

During the two discussions, circulate among the groups and gather direct quotes with the help of the scribes. Categorize the quotes by placing them in an *unlabeled* t-chart that has a column designated for endostory readings and a column designated for exostory readings. (You'll present the t-chart unlabeled so that readers can try to extrapolate the categories using the quotes.) You may notice that there are more of one kind of reading or the other for each text, which could be an interesting point to discuss. There's no need to find the same number of quotes for each category; if you have more than one for each category, that should be enough to extrapolate the two categories. If the scribes are typing quotes in a shared digital document, you can simply copy the quotes from that document and paste them into a t-chart in another part of that same document. Table 4.1 shows an example of how this t-chart might look after you've gathered quotes from the small-group discussions. While the columns in this example are labeled, remember that the columns in your t-chart won't be labeled until later.

After the discussions, reveal the unlabeled t-chart where you've collected quotes from the group. Invite readers to examine the t-chart and try to guess what the two unspecified categories are.

Introduction of New Ideas

Reveal the hidden categories on the t-chart and define *endostory* and *exostory* readings:

♦ **Endostory**: An endostory reading treats the characters like they're real people you know and focuses on their inner thoughts, feelings, and motivations. This kind of reading helps us enter the characters' universe.

◆ **Exostory**: An exostory reading treats the story like it is an object that was intentionally created by one or more people for a purpose. This kind of reading helps us understand why and how a text was made.

Concept Mapping: After defining the terms, have readers review the t-chart again to get a sense of how the two reading stances differ. Then, share a series of adjectives and have readers discuss which kind of reading those adjectives describe. (In most cases, arguments could be made to apply these adjectives to either stance.)

◆ Analytical
◆ Interesting
◆ Critical
◆ Absorbing
◆ Gossipy
◆ Nerdy
◆ Fun
◆ Intellectual
◆ Emotional

If time permits, share an excerpt of a text discussion to illustrate the difference between endostory and exostory readings (a pop culture podcast episode would be a great choice!). Invite readers to identify which parts of the conversation are endostory and which are exostory.

Major Work of the Lesson

Explain that our goal in these lessons is to bring to the surface our own tendencies as readers so that we can become more aware and intentional going forward. Emphasize that, as readers, we all take both reading stances—endostory and exostory—at one time or another. We don't need to try to make ourselves read a certain way every time. But, by becoming more aware of our reading stances, we can make more deliberate decisions about how we read stories to best suit our purposes.

Introduce the inquiry that the class will begin in this lesson. For this inquiry, students will call to mind recent readings of texts, categorize our readings as endostory or exostory, and reflect on why we may have read them one way or the other.

Invite readers to record titles or descriptions of narrative texts they've engaged with in and out of school. The academic texts might include literary texts, nonfiction texts that present a true story, historical accounts, and so forth. The personal texts might include songs, TV shows, movies, social media content, or video games.

Students reflect on their readings of each narrative text. Encourage them to call to mind what they've thought about as they've read those texts, as well as how they've discussed them with others. Students informally write whether they think their readings of each text have been mostly endostory, mostly exostory, or a combination of both. Offer some guiding questions to support their reflections:

◆ Do you find yourself thinking or talking about the characters or people in this story as if they're real people you know? (endostory)

◆ Do you find yourself wondering about why the story was written or presented the way it was? (exostory)

◆ Did the text make you feel something—did it give you butterflies in your stomach, did it make you tear up, did it make you want to stand up and shout? (endostory)

◆ Did the text give you a thought about the person or people who created the text? (exostory)

◆ Have you been asked to respond to the story in a particular way? If so, who asked you to do so, and why? What kind of reading did they encourage?

Closing and Reflection

Invite students to share some of their initial reflections in partnerships and small groups and discuss any patterns they notice (for example, if they tend to read a particular genre one way). Students may also discuss the following:

◆ Which way of reading is more fun?

◆ Which way of reading helps you understand the text better?

◆ Which way of reading helps you be a more critical reader?

Assign students to continue their inquiry by adding three more entries to their record over the next week. Remind students that the narrative texts they add can be either academic or personal. Frame this work within the larger goal: to bring to the surface our own tendencies as readers so that we can become more aware and intentional going forward.

Remixes

Teach this lesson as a standalone lesson. Drop this lesson into the final stretch of any humanities unit in which students have been engaging with multiple narrative texts. Narrative texts could be literary or narrative nonfiction texts. When students reflect on their initial inquiry, add guiding questions that can help them recognize how they read different kinds of texts differently:

- ◆ What reading stance did you mostly take when you read texts in this unit: endostory or exostory?
- ◆ Did you read certain genres of text in this unit one way, and other genres another way? Why might that have been?
- ◆ Were your tendencies in this unit the same as in past units in this subject area or different?
- ◆ Are your tendencies in this subject area the same as or different from your tendencies in other subject areas?

These questions will help readers think metacognitively about how they approach the specific topics, issues, and disciplines represented in the unit.

Embed ideas from this lesson into other lessons: Narrow the focus of this lesson to the idea that there are two major reading stances we take when we engage with narrative: endostory and exostory. Introduce and define these two stances. After readers have finished reading a narrative text, have them reflect on the stance they took as they read it. Facilitate a discussion of why they read the text the way they did and the advantages and disadvantages to each stance. After the stances have been introduced and defined, this reflection and discussion can be added onto any narrative reading experience at any point.

Lesson 4: Reading Strategically Using Multimodality and Intertextuality

In this two-day lesson, students engage with two shared pop culture texts. In the first lesson, they apply the concepts and strategies of multimodality, and, in the second lesson, they apply the concepts and skills of intertextuality. To identify promising texts for the two days of this lesson, poll the class in advance, asking them to submit some texts they'd be interested in reflecting on and analyzing together. The best texts would be familiar and high-interest to a majority of students; lengthy enough to sustain reflection and discussion; and shaped by multimodality and intertextuality, respectively.

This lesson gives students a shared context in which to explore their own reading strategies. The lesson opens with an opportunity for students to watch themselves as they engage with the day's text. They'll note the thought processes they bring to the text naturally. They then learn the terminology associated with multimodality on the first day and intertextuality on the second. Finally, they apply the concepts and skills associated with that set of terms to their own thought processes. The hope is that this lesson brings self-awareness to students' existing pop culture literacy practices. Self-awareness allows us to apply strategies with intention and sophistication.

The major work of this lesson is to analyze one's own pop culture reading strategies, drawing on the concepts and strategies associated with multimodality and intertextuality.

Opening and Invitation

To open the lesson, invite students to engage with the preselected pop culture text and annotate the text (or an artifact of the text like a transcript or a print-out of song lyrics) by recording what they're thinking at different points in the text or how they're making sense of or connecting to the meaning. Students share their annotations with a partner or two, comparing and contrasting their thought processes across the text.

Introduction of New Ideas

On the first day of this lesson, introduce the terminology associated with multimodality. On the second day of this lesson, introduce the terminology associated with intertextuality. In both cases, share an example of each term in action from your own reading experiences.

Day 1: Multimodality

◆ Modality: The system through which meaning is expressed; modes can be visual, linguistic, spatial, gestural, or aural; most pop culture texts are multimodal, meaning they incorporate multiple modes
◆ Modal affordances: What is possible to express through a particular mode
◆ Path through the text: The individual reader's unique process of navigating and interpreting the meaning of a multimodal text

Day 2: Intertextuality

◆ Referentiality: Explicit or implicit reference to another text
◆ Parody: Repeating the content or structure from an existing text in order to make a comment on that text
◆ Transmediation: A single story is told across different media, creating a coherent story-world

Major Work of the Lesson

Invite students to work independently and then in collaboration with a partner to apply this new terminology to their annotations of the text. The goal here is for students to see the ways in which they are already making sense of the text using the concepts and strategies described by the terminology.

Closing and Reflection

Students share their own examples of each of the terms under study.

Remixes

Teach this lesson as a standalone lesson in any humanities unit that makes use of texts shaped by multimodality and/or intertextuality. Drop this lesson into the unit early on to highlight the strategies students already use to make sense of such texts and show how these strategies can be transferred and applied to academic texts.

Embed ideas from this lesson into other lessons by dropping in definitions of any of the multimodality or intertextuality terms that are relevant to the goals of the lesson or unit and the texts under study.

Lesson 5: Reading Resolutions

In this lesson, students examine and reflect on their pop culture literacy practices and make reading resolutions. A reading resolution is a promise we make to ourselves to do something different with our reading. Reading resolutions are traditionally about how many books or pages we read over a given period of time. But resolutions can also be about the genres of texts we read, when and where we read, or even how we read.

The lesson begins with an opportunity for students to look back over the reading they've been tracking since Lesson 1, noticing the patterns in the reading they do and reflecting on what is and isn't working for them. Then, introduce the idea of a reading resolution by showing some online examples (there are specific recommendations for this in the lesson description) and then your own.

The final element of this process is for students to identify a reading mentor who can guide them in following through with their resolution. This can be someone they know personally whose reading they want to try to emulate. Students who choose a personal mentor craft a small set of questions they can ask their mentor in an informal interview. The reading mentor could also be someone whose reading practices are, in one way or another, made public. This might be a cultural critic, a podcast host, or a content creator. Students who choose this sort of remote mentor craft a small set of questions they can ask themselves as they deliberately engage with the mentor's content or commentary.

The major work of this lesson is for students to craft a reading resolution that is personally meaningful to them, identify a person who can guide them, and make a plan to follow through with their resolution.

Opening and Invitation

Students begin the lesson by reviewing the reading tracker they've been keeping since Lesson 1, taking note of patterns in when, what, and why they read and reflecting on the strategies they used across different kinds of texts. They might also notice how their actual reading compares to the typical weekday and typical weekend day they constructed in Lesson 1. Guide students to make connections between the reading patterns they notice and the concepts they learned in Lessons 2–4, specifically:

◆ Character affiliation
◆ Endostory and exostory stances
◆ Modal affordances
◆ Paths through the text
◆ Referentiality
◆ Parody
◆ Transmediation

Students share what they've noticed with a partner and discuss how they feel about the different kinds of reading they do in a typical week.

Introduction of New Ideas

Introduce the idea of a reading resolution: a reading resolution is a promise we make to ourselves to do something different with our reading. Illustrate the idea by sharing some examples from social media, podcasts, and news outlets. Users who participate in the TikTok subcommunity BookTok, for example, sometimes share reading resolutions, and the social media platform GoodReads hosts reading resolution discussions at the beginning of the year. You might also find reading resolution inspiration (if not reading resolutions, as such) in podcasts like *Life Kit* (Limbong, 2024) or *Pop Culture Happy Hour* (Holmes et al., 2024).

Explain the role of a reading mentor, emphasizing that a reading mentor serves as an example of the kind of reader you want to be.

◆ A reading mentor might read the kinds of texts you want to read more of

◆ They might read in the ways you want to read—for certain purposes or using certain strategies

◆ A reading mentor can be someone you know personally or someone who has made their reading public (e.g., through their social media presence, a podcast, a column in a news outlet)

◆ We can engage with mentors we know by informally interviewing them about their reading practices

◆ We can engage with public mentors by deliberately examining their work and identifying texts or practices we want to incorporate into our own reading

To support students in setting and keeping their reading resolutions, show them your own example of a reading resolution and the mentor reader who inspired or shaped it (see example in Table 4.2).

Major Work of the Lesson

In this part of the lesson, students make reading resolutions, identify a reading mentor, and make a plan to engage with that mentor. Support this work by providing a blank version of Table 4.2.

To begin, students work in partnerships to brainstorm possible reading resolutions based on their review of their week of reading. Then, students independently select and shape one reading resolution. Students reconvene with their partner to brainstorm possible reading mentors who can inspire or shape their reading resolution. Encourage students to think broadly about possible mentors, reminding them that a mentor reader can be someone they know personally or someone whose

TABLE 4.2 Model of reading resolutions.

Reading Resolution: Listen to a Wider Variety of Music

What is my reading resolution?	My music resolution is to not rely on my Spotify on-repeat playlist when I listen to music during the day. Instead, I resolve to create a playlist called "New Songs" and add 3–5 songs that are new to me each week. At the end of each week, I'll decide which songs to keep on the list and which to delete. I'll make this my default playlist for when I'm commuting, running errands, or doing chores.
Why does this resolution matter to me?	I really love music, but I get stuck in a rut with the songs I listen to. I realize that I use songs to transport me to particular daydreams, which is fine sometimes. But I also want to listen to songs more mindfully and appreciate the craft that went into them. It's tempting to only listen to what's comfortable and what helps me feel a certain way, but I don't want that to be the only reason I listen to music.
Who can be a mentor to me in this resolution, and what would make them a good mentor?	Nate Sloan. Nate Sloan is a musicologist who hosts the podcast *Switched on Pop* (Sloan & Harding, 2014-present). In that podcast, he and a guest dissect new music, exploring how the songs were crafted and how they connect to other songs, genres, and the culture more generally.
When and how can I engage with my mentor?	I can engage with my mentor by listening to his podcast and following him on social media. I can follow his analysis of songs closely to think up ways I can appreciate and enjoy new songs. I can also possibly select some of the songs he features on the podcast for my "New Songs" playlist.
What questions might I *ask* of this mentor, either in conversation or in examination of their public work?	When I listen to an episode of *Switched on Pop*, I can ask myself: ◆ What elements of the song's craft does he notice and highlight in his analysis? ◆ What connections does he make between this song and other songs? To the culture more generally? ◆ What does he seem to like and enjoy about this song?

reading practices are documented and shared online. Once students have made a selection, they develop a plan to communicate with that mentor.

Closing and Reflection

Students share their reading resolutions and mentor engagement plans publicly with the class. Consider having students submit this information in an online form or shared document. Preview the class's reading resolution accountability plan, which should include a handful of preset check-ins on progress toward resolutions and at least one opportunity to share what they learned from their mentor after engaging with them.

Remixes

Teach this lesson as a standalone lesson by inviting students to make reading resolutions at the beginning of the school year, the marking period, or a new unit. Preview the academic goals of upcoming instruction and discuss how the academic work might intersect with their personal reading practices, pop culture and otherwise. Then, guide students to set reading resolutions that bridge their academic and personal reading. For example, if you're studying 19th century British literature in an upcoming unit, a student might set a reading resolution to watch film adaptations of that literature and examine how contemporary culture shaped the adaptations of those works. Or if you're studying the structure of the US federal government, a student might set a reading resolution to find current social media content that comments on, critiques, or even satirizes the different branches of government.

Embed ideas from this lesson into other lessons by having students reflect on their reading and make resolutions or set goals for themselves. You might have students do this after they read one major text and before they start the next one, or you might have them do this when they reflect on their learning at the end of a unit. If students are learning to write literary analysis, have them examine models of literary analyses and extrapolate what the writer might have done *while they read* to produce this analysis. Encourage students to try out that kind of reading themselves.

Final Note: Reading Is Reading

This chapter's lessons are all about helping young people develop self-awareness and intentionality in their pop culture reading practices. These lessons teach students a lot about pop culture literacy—from character affiliation to reading stances, from modal affordances to parody to transmediation—and students will likely not develop total mastery of all of these concepts and strategies in these lessons. That's okay, because the broader purpose of these lessons is to shift students' mindsets, to help them see that the *reading* they do in school is not so different from, or doesn't have to be so different from, the reading they do at home. We can set goals, apply strategies, and modulate our reading to make for richer, more mindful, and more pleasurable experiences with all kinds of texts.

References

Carpenter, S. (2024). Espresso [Song]. On *Short n' sweet*. Island Records.

Chenn, A. [antonychenn]. (2022, April 24). We fought every single boss in *Genshin impact* [Video]. YouTube. www.youtube.com/watch?v=lnxFskQk2il

Duke, N. K., & Cartwright, K. B. (2021). The science of reading progresses: Communicating advances beyond the simple view of reading. *Reading Research Quarterly*, *56*(S1), S25–S44. https://doi.org/10.1002/rrq.411

Holmes, L., Thompson, S., Weldon, G., & Harris, A. (2024, January 1). Our 2024 pop culture resolutions [Audio podcast episode]. In *Pop culture happy hour*. NPR. www.npr.org/2024/01/01/1197959254/our-2024-pop-culture-resolutions

Limbong, A. (Host). (2024, April 30). How to practice deep reading [Audio podcast episode]. In *Life kit*. NPR. www.npr.org/2024/04/30/1196979151/how-to-practice-deep-reading

Matter, J. (2024, May 11). Saying yes to the most spoiled kid in America for 24 hours [Video]. YouTube. www.youtube.com/watch?v=t8twhAWPLX0

Porter, K., & Adejuyigbe, D. (Hosts). (2014–2017). *Gilmore guys* [Audio podcast]. Headgum.

Porter, K., & Adejuyigbe, D. (Hosts). (2015). 522—A house is not a home [Audio podcast episode]. In *Gilmore Guys*. Headgum. https://headgum.com/gilmore-guys/522-a-house-is-not-a-home-with-aisha-muharrar

Sherman-Palladino, A. (Writer & Director). (2005, May 17). A house is not a home (Season 4, Episode 22) [TV series episode]. In *Gilmore girls*. Dorothy Parker Drank Here Productions; Warner Bros. Television.

Sloan, N., & Harding, C. (Hosts). (2014–present). *Switched on pop* [Podcast]. New York Magazine; Vox Media. https://switchedonpop.com/

Still Watching Netflix. (2022). *Wednesday Addams being the ultimate mood* [Video]. YouTube. www.youtube.com/watch?v=Y2WdFQCE0Z8

Syfret, W. (2019, September 18). From *Succession* to *The Bold Type*: How recap culture made us love television more. *The Guardian*. www.theguardian.com/commentisfree/2019/sep/19/from-succession-to-the-bold-type-how-recap-culture-made-us-love-television-more

5

Layers of Story

Hidden Stories

This chapter is about finding hidden stories in texts, even texts that aren't explicitly narrative. The idea of hidden meanings isn't new: that every text is attended by subtext, that the outer story of what characters or people are doing illuminates an inner story of deeper significance, that there's meaning to be found even beyond what the author intended. As teachers, we often encourage young people to read texts in search of these hidden meanings. In this chapter, I hope to show that we shouldn't restrict this search to the meanings of the texts themselves. Instead, we should push ourselves and our students toward interpretations that illuminate something bigger about ourselves, others, and the world around us.

In this chapter, a *story* is not necessarily an individual narrative text; it's a quality that imbues all texts. Interpreting layers of story, then, involves seeing the way the world has worked its way into the text, implanting its narrative logic through storylines and character tropes. When we read a story over and over—meaning, when we read the same *story* across

DOI: 10.4324/9781032667027-8

multiple texts—each reading reinscribes, and deepens, the ideas and logic of that story.

For example, I've read the story of a plucky straight single woman protagonist finding her way (and herself) in the big city countless times. I read that story in *Sex and the City* (Star, 1998–2004), in articles about apartment hunting in the *New York Times* column The Hunt (e.g., Cohen, 2024), in memes about the discontents of heterosexual arrangements, and in my friends' dating lore. What ideas might that story reinscribe in its reader? Perhaps that life for people like me takes a certain shape, is bent toward certain outcomes, is marked by certain signifiers of success, comfort, and belonging. When we read actively, critically, and strategically, we first recognize the story, and then we engage in it, analyze and interpret it, connect it to ideas beyond itself, situate it within what we know about society, reflect on our relationship to it, develop a perspective on it, and, if we so choose, resist it.

Finding Mentors: Drunk Barry Jenkins Live-Tweeting *Notting Hill*

In 2018, acclaimed film director Barry Jenkins live-tweeted the film *Notting Hill* (Curtis & Michell, 1999), viewed sans audio over the shoulder of his seatmate on a transatlantic flight. His reading of the film was "helped along" (his words) by consumption of Woodford Reserve bourbon. While I'm going to offer a curiously specific and reverential account of these tweets, they're exactly as scattered and unformed as you'd expect, given these circumstances. Yet, I suggest that the work he's doing to read the story within the film is exactly the kind of work we'd want to teach young people to do. Drunk Barry Jenkins live-tweeting *Notting Hill*, therefore, is our mentor reader.

To understand his reading, I'll borrow two concepts from Chapter 2: *storylines* and *character tropes*. Storylines, according to Søndergaard (2002), are naturalized, conventional cultural narratives that create identities and can serve to explain what people do, why, and to what effect. The second concept, *character tropes*, refers to naturalized, conventional figures in such stories. We recognize character tropes by their surfaces—identity markers, appearance and dress, and basic function in the story—and project assumed inner worlds of desires, motivations, and traits into them. With these concepts in mind, let's join Jenkins on his journey across the Atlantic and through the classic 90s romcom *Notting Hill*.

Storylines

Notting Hill tells the story of movie star Anna Scott (Julia Roberts) who falls for a modest bookshop owner William Thacker (Hugh Grant) in the Notting Hill neighborhood of London. Jenkins begins with the basic premise that Julia Roberts is supremely attractive in this film: "STUNNING," he says. He makes the point best later, when he evocatively describes her as "a lamp you find in some antique shop in Nova Scotia. A bulb rather. With infinite lumens and a millionwatt range. . . . There was a time when this woman's smile could literally replenish you." Given this assessment, Jenkins wonders what Julia Roberts (Anna) is doing with Hugh Grant (William). "Julia just looks waaaaaaaay too much for his character in this!" he tweets. He wonders if Hugh Grant has a particular kind of romantic and sexual prowess he comes to refer to as "English Cat Game."

Since he can't hear the audio, Jenkins relies on multimodal and intertextual elements of the film, as well as responses to his tweets, to resolve this basic conundrum. "Okay somebody tweeted me that Hugh owns a bookstore," he reports, but counters that owning a bookstore is not enough to make one worthy of Anna who "had that braid AND that onesie body suit tucked into jeans and flat heel boots . . . basically Jay-Lo [sic] on IN LIVING COLOR!" In other words, too much for William. "[H]e better be spitting some SERIOUS English Cat Game." In the final act of the film, William and his ragtag group of family and friends rush to a press conference so he can declare his love before Anna departs for the US "THAT'S RIGHT HUGH HUMBLE YOSELF!!!" Jenkins opines. "That's Julia Roberts bruh, chase you must!!!!"

Jenkins gradually makes sense of the Anna–William pairing. He first draws on Anna's growing comfort with William to explain why she might want to be with him:

> Julia Roberts on a roof in Notting Hill. In Hugh Grants sweatshirt on a roof in Notting Hill. Little to no makeup. Reebok trainers. Wow. If I were Julia and I saw myself in the mirror, SAW MYSELF looking that way, FEELING that comfortable? Okay THEN . . . then I would get it.

And later:

> Okay so Hugh is in his bookstore now and as a lover of books and a believer of miracles I can see, I can FINALLY FULLY see how Julia Roberts as Jenny From The Block fell for this English Cat Game, I salute you book slinging grey Oxford wearing remnants of shaving Hugh Grant.

By the time William and friends are rushing to the press conference, Jenkins, like viewers the world over, is rooting for the pair.

Character Tropes

We see two character tropes in Jenkins's reading of the film. First up is the English Cat. The English Cat is a mild-mannered, sometimes bumbling, often floppy-haired, ostensibly ineffectual man who is nevertheless romantically successful with women. (Hugh Grant played the trope often and well in the 1990s.) The English Cat's "game," so to speak, is rooted in his literary sensibility, gentle wit, and distinctly English charm—a kind of charm that presumably only reads as such in the US. It doesn't matter if the English Cat lacks some of the traditional markers of masculinity thought to appeal to straight women. Jenkins, for example, makes a meal of the fact that Hugh Grant is shown shaving, when "everybody knows that HUGH GRANT DONT SHAVE!!!!"

In appreciation of Jenkins's vivid description, we'll call the second character trope the Millionwatt Bulb. The Millionwatt Bulb is the supremely attractive woman who is the object of male desire, attraction, and romantic longing. The Millionwatt Bulb has a smile that will, as Jenkins says, "literally replenish you." There's not much else to say about this character trope because, by design, there's not much to say about this character trope. She is desirable and therefore desired. She is the thing the movie happens around. The storyline is set in motion by the interaction of these two character tropes. The humble English Cat must prove his worth to the Millionwatt Bulb to have her.

Jenkins as Mentor Reader

Jenkins is able to track much of the film's plot, even though his reading is significantly constrained by a lack of audio, spotty in-flight Wi-Fi, the distraction of Twitter, and bourbon. He finds the story in the text—with great relish—by moving between endostory and exostory stances and by reading multimodally, intertextually, and socially.

Endostory and Exostory Readings. Jenkins takes an endostory stance as he questions, speculates about, and eventually comes to accept Anna's attraction to William. He moves into an exostory stance when he comments on and compliments the work of the director, costume designer, makeup artist, and script supervisor. His insider knowledge of the film industry and expertise is on display in these exostory comments:

> At first I thought it was too cute a tell to reduce her makeup as she grew comfortable with him but they stuck to it and it's subtle and just superb. Hats off to script sup and make up artist there.

And: "After peeping these dolly/zoom combos in this dinner scene I looked up the director and OF COURSE it's Roger Michell!!! a G and a Gent."

Multimodal Reading. Jenkins reads the text multimodally. Without access to the film's aural and linguistic features, Jenkins relies on the visual and gestural features to identify both the character tropes and the storyline. He notes many visual details in the costuming ("this Oxford two-sizes too big") and the mise-en-scene ("What kind of bookstore owner has a flat like THAT in NOTTING HILL?"). And he reads the film gesturally, noting and wondering about meaningful micro-actions ("his hand on her back") and facial expressions ("Julia shot him that brow!!!").

Intertextual Reading. Jenkins also makes sense of the film intertextually. He reads the costuming by comparing Anna's look in one scene to Jennifer Lopez's in *In Living Color* (1990–1994) and in another to her character in *Pretty Woman* (1990), saying she looks "a weeeeeeee bit PRETTY WOMAN but I didn't say that." He also creates his own intertextual assemblage by listening to Rick Ross's (2012) "Hold me Back" as he watches along, claiming that it's "THE primo soundtrack" for the movie." He later marvels that his iTunes playlist is beginning to sync with the movie when DJ Shadow's lush, atmospheric song "Six Days" (2002) comes on, just as Anna is shown floating through outer space (acting in a movie within the movie) after a break-up with William.

The most obvious form of intertextuality, however, is in his recognition of the storyline itself. Jenkins, like all viewers, comes to the movie with the storyline already in place; it is the framework into which all of the specifics of the film are poured. He understands the film as primarily about a romantic chase: the English Cat chases the Millionwatt Bulb. The chase must be thwarted at several points by circumstance, misunderstanding, and bad actors before crescendoing into a literal chase ("chase you must!!!!"). And, of course, the chase must end in a committed romantic partnership. This storyline—sturdy and recognizable as it is—allows Jenkins to follow the plot despite significant constraints and distractions.

Social Reading. Jenkins constructs and negotiates meaning in conversation with others, drawing on Twitter responses to understand William's appeal and, at one point, polling his followers to clarify whose hand was on whose back.

There's much to learn from—and, I think, appreciate in—Jenkins's reading of *Notting Hill*. More than anything, it serves as a powerful counterargument to the assumption that being strategic or even analytical in our pop culture reading saps all the joy and pleasure from the experience. It seems to me that Jenkins's joy and pleasure are only enhanced by his analysis. I see a mind turned all the way on, a sophisticated reader of films bringing all of his knowledge of how stories go and how films are made to his viewing. Of course, in *Notting Hill*, the story isn't exactly hiding, or, if it is, it's hiding in plain sight. But Jenkins doesn't just find the story of William and Anna in the film. He finds broader cultural narratives about the dynamics of heteroromantic relationships.

Lessons on Layers of Story

Sociologist Arthur Frank (2012) argues that there is no such thing as experience, or even reality, without story. Conventionally, we assume that storytelling goes like this: something happens, and then later we tell a story about it. In this conventional framework, story is mimetic; it imitates the experience it describes (p. 34). But Frank and others have argued that our bone-deep understanding of story is what shapes the isolated, otherwise meaningless *events* of life into *experience*.

Without story, my fingers are clacking on a keyboard, and letters are appearing on a screen. With story, I'm toiling and striving, thinking important thoughts, fashioning them into sentences, pushing against the tide of digital distractions and the tyranny of the commonsense, a lone writer in a cruel world communing with her essential self and reaching—straining—for inspiration and insight. This is to say that what is happening is not, in and of itself, an *experience*. It's the story I tell myself that makes it an experience.

In this way, the stories we tell and the stories we encounter take on a mutually reinforcing relationship. The stories we encounter make sense because of our experiences, and our experiences make sense because of the stories we encounter. And, of course, as we saw in Barry Jenkins's (2018) *Notting Hill* live-tweet, the stories we encounter make sense because of the other stories we've encountered.

Proceeding from this premise, story is incredibly powerful—and perilous. At its worst, it can amplify ideas and messages that make life in the social world more challenging, even untenable. Story can marginalize. It can constrain our sense of possibility and appetite for social change. It can persuade us against our own inherent worth. So what might we teach young people about story? What does it mean to be an active, critical, and strategic reader and writer of story? First and foremost, we must put students on the search for story: in pop culture texts, in digital media, in academic texts, and in their own storytelling. We should help them find the stories that are reiterated and rearticulated across texts, contexts, and time and examine the deeper ideas—ideas about ourselves, others, and the world—that they reify and animate.

In Lesson 1, students explore their own storytelling, taking note of how a moment of life morphs as we tell stories about it. In Lessons 2–3, students learn about the concepts of *storylines* and *character tropes*, the top and therefore most easily recognizable layer of the stories embedded in texts. In Lesson 4, they begin to connect the stories they tell to the stories they read and hear out in the world, exploring and testing the limits of the idea that story constitutes experience. Finally, Lesson 5 directs students' attention to the site where stories circulate, intersect, converge, and reinforce each other: social media. In this final lesson of the sequence, students apply the story concepts they've learned to social media content and reflect on how these concepts might help them engage with social media more actively, critically, and strategically.

Lesson 1: Generating Stories of Personal Experience

The purpose of this lesson is to invite students into an exploration of stories. This lesson grounds that exploration in students' own stories of personal experience and involves two major learning experiences. First, they flash-draft—or quickly write without judgment or revision—several stories of personal experience, guided by teacher prompts. Then, they participate in a story "speed dating" activity. In this activity, students choose one of their flash-draft stories and tell it several times in a row to different partners. This learning experience concludes with a rewrite of the story they told and a reflection. Students take note of the similarities and differences between their original flash draft and their new draft and reflect on how and when their story changed—or stayed the same—over the course of the speed-dating experience.

The major work of this lesson is to develop curiosity about how and why stories sometimes change, sometimes stay the same, and, either way, shape our understanding of our lives.

Opening and Invitation

Launch this sequence of lessons by inviting students into an opening reflection on these questions:

- ◆ What was the last story you heard, watched, or read?
- ◆ Where and when did you hear, watch, or read it?
- ◆ What was the last story you told, wrote, or created?
- ◆ Where and when did you tell, write, or create it?

Students reflect first in writing and then share some of these stories, in brief, with the whole class. As students share, chart up the stories so that you can build a sizable and varied list of stories.

Ask the class: what would you say is true of *all* of these stories? What common qualities or features do these stories, and all stories, have?

Introduction of New Ideas

Highlight the following points, building on students' comments in the previous discussion:

- ◆ We know we can find stories in the traditional places: movies, TV shows, short stories, and novels. But, over the next few lessons, we'll come to see that stories are everywhere
- ◆ We'll explore how stories shape the way we think about and understand ourselves, others, and the world around us. We're not always consciously aware of how stories are

affecting us. That's why stories are worth our attention and study
◆ To do this work, we'll want to become a magnet for stories. We'll live life over the next couple of weeks looking for the stories in everything

Major Work of the Lesson

Flash-Drafting. Explain that we'll start our exploration with our own stories—and we'll end with our own stories too. Lead students in a 15-minute period of flash-drafting. In flash-drafting, students write quickly without stopping to judge what they're writing or check that it would make sense to others. The idea is to get out as much writing as possible. Students flash-write several stories of recent experience. Consider helping students elicit story ideas using the prompts in Table 5.1 (or your own favorite story-generating prompts!).

Speed Dating. Facilitate a 20-minute "speed dating" exercise. In speed dating, we line up two rows of chairs facing each other. Students sit facing each other knee-to-knee, and one of the rows rotates every minute or so to a new partner. In this exercise,

TABLE 5.1 Storytelling prompts inspired by *This American Life*.

Storytelling Prompts

Useful storytelling prompts help us surface surprising and fresh story topics from our well of personal experience. A prompt that's useful for one person might not be as useful for the next, so it's best to sit with a few different possible prompts to see what works. The prompts below were adapted from the themes of recent episodes of the podcast *This American Life* (Glass, 1995–present). You might also try reverse-engineering prompts from stories you encounter and enjoy.

◆ Tell a story about a time you felt unprepared for something that happened
◆ Tell a story about something you did that seemed like a good idea at the time
◆ Tell a story about something that someone did or said too soon
◆ Tell a story about a time when you couldn't find the words to say what you needed to say
◆ Tell a story about a time you saw yourself in a new way
◆ Tell a story about something you wanted to quit doing—but couldn't
◆ Tell a story about a time when you "left the fold," or left a close group you were a part of

students choose one of the stories they flash-drafted and tell it again and again to different partners. In the first half of the exercise, the students who rotate are the ones telling their stories; in the second half of the exercise, the students who are sitting still tell their stories. The purpose of this exercise is to notice how the same story can morph—or not—with repeated tellings. Students select one of the stories they wrote, whichever feels most interesting and/or best-developed.

Explain the exercise, set up the chairs for speed-dating, and invite students to begin. Facilitate the experience by cueing students to rotate to the next partner after a preset period of time.

After the speed dating exercise, students rewrite the story they told. Then, students reflect:

- ◆ What are the similarities and differences between the original flash draft of your story and the new draft?
- ◆ What did you notice as you told the story over and over? When and how did it change? Did it get more different or more similar over time?

Closing and Reflection

Facilitate a reflective discussion about the flash-drafting and speed-dating exercises. Ask: what did these exercises help you understand about stories that you didn't understand before? (Students may note that the same story can be told in different ways or that crafting and telling a story changes the memory of the experience, or they may note patterns in the kinds of stories that their classmates told.)

Remixes

Teach this lesson as a standalone lesson at the beginning of a unit on personal narrative, personal essay, or memoir writing. In this context, the lesson can help students access possible story or essay ideas and moments of significance from their lives.

Embed ideas from this lesson into other lessons. The flash-drafting exercise can be used early in any literacy or English unit. Flash-drafting can help students generate and begin to develop ideas for writing. The speed-dating exercise can be used across content areas to illustrate how any human account of an event can shape our memory and understanding of that event. It can also reinforce the idea that the storyteller's perspective and positioning affects how a story is told.

Lesson 2: Articulating Storylines

The purpose of this lesson is to help attune students to the latent stories in all kinds of texts, whether explicitly narrative or not. The lesson introduces the concept of *storylines*, adapted here from Søndergaard's (2002) concept. In this lesson, storylines are defined as familiar plot arcs that repeat across cultural texts. Storylines help us explain what people do, why they do it, and to what effect. The lesson opens with an invitation to explore multiple examples of storylines in short narrative video clips. This exercise illustrates to students that they already *know* storylines, even if they don't know they know them.

In the lesson, students practice articulating storylines they see across a variety of texts. (Note that this lesson does *not* include memes, as that particular genre is reserved for Lesson 5.) We ask students to articulate them in 15 words or fewer for an important reason: storylines are, more than anything, *simple*. That's what allows them to be repeated across texts and contexts. Articulating a storyline, then, requires that we strip away the specifics of a particular text and allow the skeleton of the story to emerge.

The major work of this lesson is to identify and articulate a storyline latent in at least one pop culture and one academic text.

Opening and Invitation

To invite students into this first day of story analysis, show three short narrative videos. These videos present self-contained stories that align to popular storylines. I recommend choosing simple short films like *One Small Step* (Pontillas & Chesworth, 2018) or *Piper* (Barillaro, 2016). Before the final beat of each video, pause it and ask students to imagine and discuss what they think will happen at the end.

After engaging in these three videos, ask: how did you know what would happen at the end of each video? (Students may note similarity between the stories presented in these videos and other stories they've engaged with in the past.)

Frame the lesson by explaining that we'll turn our attention to stories we read rather than our own stories we write or tell. We'll analyze the kinds of stories we find in pop culture, in literature, in other subjects in school, and in our daily lives.

Introduction of New Ideas

Share the following quote about stories from Frank (2012): "Stories echo other stories, with those echoes adding force to the present story" (p. 57). Offer a new way to think about stories by highlighting the following points:

- Stories don't simply represent a set of events, fictional or real
- Instead, as Frank suggests, stories connect to and amplify other stories
- Another way to look at stories is as different versions of one basic story
- Stories help us understand our experiences, and our experiences help us understand stories

Define *storylines*: Familiar plot arcs that repeat across cultural texts. Explain that storylines help us explain what people do, why they do it, and to what effect. Connect storylines to an example from the opening of the lesson. For example, the storyline of *Piper* (Barillaro, 2016) could be "child overcomes fear with the help of a special friend." Invite students to consider other versions of that same story they've seen and heard elsewhere.

Offer a new storyline: "Boy meets girl. Boy falls for girl. Girl pulls away. Boy wins her back." Invite students to discuss texts that include this storyline.

Major Work of the Lesson

Frame the learning experience: In this activity, we'll look at two examples of stories in texts that aren't explicitly narrative. One will be a pop culture text, and the other will be an academic text. The challenge of this experience is to find the storylines in these texts. Remember that storylines are simple plot arcs. When we tell a storyline, we remove all of the specifics of the text to find just the familiar plot arc that's repeated across lots of different texts. We should aim to tell the storyline back in no more than 15 words.

Invite students to read and analyze one pop culture text and one academic text to find the storylines layered within them. Table 5.2 shows a small set of examples of text pairs and their storylines.

If time permits, invite students to repeat this activity with two self-selected texts: one text they read because they had to and one they read because they chose to. Throughout this learning experience, coach students to reduce the storylines they see to their simplest form. Publicly document their attempts to articulate the storylines in the room.

Closing and Reflection

Students revisit the story they wrote in the previous lesson and reflect on whether there's a storyline embedded in the story. Invite students to articulate the storyline in their own story in 15 words or fewer.

Remixes

Teach this lesson as a standalone lesson in any humanities unit that emphasizes concepts related to cultural allegories or

TABLE 5.2 Examples of texts and their storylines.

Pop Culture Texts and Storylines	Academic Texts and Storylines
Text: "Driver's License" (Rodrigo, 2021)	**Text:** *Buzz Aldrin on the Moon with the American Flag* (NASA, 1969)
Storyline: Boy makes and breaks promises. Girl obsesses endlessly.	**Storyline:** The US's destiny is to expand, conquer, and claim.
Text: Stanley Cup	**Text:** 2004 Democratic National Convention Keynote Address (Obama, 2004)
Storyline: Only the coolest kids' parents buy them the thing that everyone has.	**Storyline:** We can all love each other even though we're different and we disagree.

mythologies, stereotypes and archetypes, or the conventions of Western storytelling. This lesson can be used to highlight what the same basic plot arc can look like across disparate texts and across history. Select shared texts for the opening and the major work that suit the particularities of the content area and unit.

Embed ideas from this lesson into other lessons. The notion of a *storyline* can be introduced and applied in any humanities unit in which students investigate conventional storytelling, whether in a literary context or a broader sociocultural context.

Lesson 3: Identifying and Analyzing Character Tropes

In this lesson, students continue their exploration of the latent layers of story in texts of all kinds. In the previous lesson, they uncovered storylines—or familiar, conventionalized plot arcs— in a range of texts. In this lesson, they uncover *character tropes*, or recognizable character types or categories, that repeat across cultural texts. The purpose of this lesson is not only to identify the character tropes that are in play in a given text but also to connect character tropes with storylines.

The major work of this lesson is to consider and discuss which character tropes go with which storylines. In other words, what kinds of stories do we tend to tell about these different kinds of characters? By the end of the lesson, students will be able to identify and retell stories that place character tropes within storylines.

Opening and Invitation

To open the lesson, have students engage in a multimodal exploration of character tropes in pop culture. Share a range of relatable character trope examples from across an expanse of time to illustrate the endurance of these tropes. You might share clips from TV shows, movies, video games, songs, or music videos.

As the class engages with the examples, chart up the names of the character tropes and some of their key inner and outer characteristics. Guide students to read the character tropes featured in these examples multimodally, paying attention to their style of dress, movement and mannerisms, speech, and the physical setting of their interactions. In some of the clips, the tropes are explicitly named. You can find an example of what this chart might look like in Table 5.3.

Introduction of New Ideas

Teach new concepts and terms to help explain the character tropes they just saw in the pop culture examples. Define character tropes: recognizable character types or categories that repeat across cultural texts. Explain the relationship between character tropes and storylines using an analogy: storylines are to plot as character tropes are to characters. Connect the definition

TABLE 5.3 Examples of character tropes in pop culture texts, 1985–2024.

Text	Trope	Characteristics
The Breakfast Club (Hughes, 1985)	"Brain"/Nerd (Brian)	Nerdy, smart, deferential toward authority, conflict-avoidant
	"Princess" (Claire)	Spoiled, self-centered, wealthy, secretly dissatisfied with life
	"Athlete"/Jock (Andrew)	Tough, intimidating, under pressure to perform
Clueless (Heckerling, 1995)	Lovable ditz (Cher)	Pretty, upbeat, charming, shallow, unconcerned about the world
	Ugly duckling (Tai)	Eccentric, not conscious of image, in need of help
"You Belong with Me" (White, 2008)	Quiet artsy girl (played by Swift)	Sweet, shy, creative, intellectually deep
	Cheerleader (played by Swift in a wig)	Popular, bold, sexually forward, invested in social status
Glee (Murphy, 2009–2015)	Type-A leader (Rachel)	Ruthless, self-centered, uncaring, goal-oriented
	Fallen good girl (Quinn)	Image-conscious, conflicted, desperate
Mean Girls (Jayne & Perez, 2024)	"Corny Horny Band Freaks"	Nerdy, sexually active, interested in niche hobbies
	"Classic Burn-Outs"	Alternative, dazed, laid-back, unconcerned
	"Plastics"	Popular, superficial, image-conscious, exclusive

of character tropes to the examples students just explored. You may need to highlight the similarities and differences between character tropes and other terms they may have heard or used in the past, such as *stereotypes* and *archetypes*.

Share the framing questions that we'll consider and discuss for the remainder of the lesson and invite students to reflect privately and informally in writing on one or more of these questions.

◆ Who gets to invent these categories, and who must fit themselves into them?
◆ What kinds of stories can we tell about each of these character tropes?
◆ Are character tropes harmful or empowering?

Major Work of the Lesson

Students work in small groups to connect character tropes to the storylines they articulated in the previous lesson. The goal of the activity is to determine which character tropes go with—or seem to make most sense within—which storylines.

In small groups, students select a storyline they articulated in the previous lesson. Then, they imagine which character trope(s) would fit in with that storyline.

They collaboratively write the story of that character in a sentence or two, inserting the character tropes into storylines. Invite groups to share the stories they crafted. You can find an example of what this work might look like in Table 5.4.

Closing and Reflection

Revisit the three framing questions presented earlier in the lesson:

◆ Who gets to invent these categories, and who must fit themselves into them?
◆ What kinds of stories can we tell about each of these character tropes?
◆ Are character tropes harmful or empowering?

TABLE 5.4 Examples of storyline–character-trope alignment.

Storyline	Character Tropes	Story
Boy makes and breaks promises. Girl obsesses endlessly.	Jock, Type-A Leader	The Jock breaks up with the Type-A Leader because he can't meet her unreasonably high expectations of him. The Type-A Leader, who truly loved him, obsesses over him and tries to get him back.
We can all love each other even though we're different and we disagree.	Princess, Corny Horny Band Freak	The Princess and the Corny Horny Band Freak are assigned to do a group project together, much to their dismay. Even though they have nothing in common, they grow to appreciate each other's unique contributions to the project and respect each other as individuals.
Young person overcomes fear with the help of a special friend.	Nerd, Lovable Ditz	The Nerd is very book-smart, but she has social anxiety and doesn't know how to navigate high school social events. The lovable ditz takes her under her wing, introduces her to new friends, and shows her there's nothing to be afraid of.

Students review what they initially wrote in reflection and then add to or update their reflection in light of the last activity. Close the lesson by inviting students to share their responses to one or more of the questions.

Remixes

Teach this lesson as a standalone lesson in any humanities unit that emphasizes concepts related to cultural allegories or mythologies, stereotypes and archetypes, or the conventions of Western storytelling. This lesson can be used to highlight what the same basic character trope can look like across disparate texts and across history. Pre-select storylines for students to work with as they make connections between character tropes and storylines.

Embed ideas from this lesson into other lessons. The notion of a *character trope* can be introduced and applied in any humanities unit in which students investigate conventional storytelling, whether in a literary context or a broader sociocultural context.

Lesson 4: Connecting the Stories We Tell to the Stories We Receive

This lesson invites students to explore the following question: how do the stories we tell connect to the stories we encounter? In Lesson 1, students generated a number of stories of their own personal experience and practiced telling one of those stories orally and in writing. In Lessons 2–3, they learned about two narrative elements—*storylines* and *character tropes*—that repeat across cultural texts. They entertained the notion that individual stories are really just different versions of a small set of larger cultural narratives. At this point in the sequence, students might be starting to consider whether any of the stories we tell or hear are truly unique. They might even be thinking about whether any of our experiences are truly unique, given the way cultural stories shape how we move through the world.

This lesson, then, connects their storytelling from Lesson 1 to their story reading and analysis from Lessons 2–3. Students revisit the stories they generated in Lesson 1 to see if there's evidence of character tropes and storylines. After a period of inquiry and exploration, students learn about the concept of *probable stories*, or the stories we improvise in conversation that can serve as the connective tissue between our stories and the stories around us.

By the end of this lesson, students will have interpreted their own stories using the lenses of *character tropes* and *storylines* and analyzed examples of how *probable stories* connect individuals' stories to larger cultural narratives.

Invitation and Opening

Introduce the idea that the use of the word *like* has changed our interpersonal storytelling. Linguist Alexandra D'Arcy explains this phenomenon in an episode of the *Decoder Ring* podcast "Mailbag: The Recorder, Limos, and 'Baby on Board' Signs" (Paskin, 2023, 18:53–24:58).

Students reflect in writing about how interpersonal storytelling might be different without the use of *like*. (Without *like*, we wouldn't be able to express what we were thinking and feeling in the moment as easily. We might not as easily find common, relatable ground with our listeners.)

Major Work of the Lesson

Pose the central question of the lesson: how do the stories we tell connect to the stories we encounter? Frame the lesson as an opportunity to understand how our own personal stories of experience fit in with the larger cultural stories we've been studying.

Students engage in an independent inquiry into their own storytelling. They examine the stories they generated in Lesson 1 looking for evidence of *storylines* (the story itself takes the shape of a storyline) and *character tropes* (the student or someone else in the story could be seen as a character trope).

After an initial period of inquiry and reflection, draw students into conversation with each other. Students share what they discovered and then consider whether—and how—storylines and character tropes help us remember, talk about, and/or understand our own experiences.

Introduction of New Ideas

Introduce the concept of a *probable story*:

◆ Probable stories are hypothetical scenarios presented as universal experiences
◆ Probable stories are improvised in conversation to help us interpret our own or others' stories
◆ Probable stories can feel true but limit the way we think about ourselves, others, and the world around us

Facilitate a collaborative read-aloud of a conversation transcript that features a probable story. (The example in the inset is adapted from the Group's discussion of the music videos presented in Chapter 1.) Guide students to notice key words that indicate a probable story is being told and consider whether the probable story is helpful or harmful in making sense of the story at hand.

Discussion Context: A, B, and C are discussing a music video that features women who are very made up and wearing revealing clothes and a man, the artist, who is dressed down. They are interpreting why the women and the man are presented so differently in the video.

> **A:** It makes sense, though. You probably see girls care more about their looks than a boy. Boys probably throw on whatever clothes and don't really care if it even all goes together. A girl is going to take a long time to get dressed. She's going to do her whole skincare routine, her makeup.
>
> **B:** She's going to try on a million different outfits before picking the right one.
>
> **A:** Right, that's right. She's going to send pics to her friends to get outfit approval. It's likely going to be a whole process.
>
> **C:** But I don't know. A boy nowadays is just as into his looks as a girl. He gets his hair done and everything, trying to look like that football player with the curly mullet. They probably brush their hair for like an hour.
>
> **B:** But still. They're most likely listening to music like this and watching these videos thinking that they don't have to look any certain way and still they can get probably whatever girl they want.

Emphasize why these conversational moves might be called *probable* stories and ask: are these stories really probable? When someone says that something *probably would* happen, is it true?

Closing and Reflection

Revisit the central question of the lesson: how do the stories we tell connect to the stories we receive? Students reflect on and discuss this question in light of both their inquiry and the example of a probable story they reviewed.

Remixes

Teach this lesson as a standalone lesson by dropping it into a unit on personal narrative, personal essay, or memoir writing. Teach the lesson after students have produced a draft and use it as the impetus for a round of revision, focused on making their drafts fresher and more original or on incorporating a reflective narrative voice.

Embed ideas from this lesson into other lessons using the lesson's central question: how do the stories we tell connect to the stories we encounter? This question can be used to spark and guide discussion of the larger topic of storytelling, whether literary, journalistic, or historical storytelling.

Lesson 5: Social Media Storytelling

By this point, students have studied the stories layered into a range of texts. These texts have varied by type, genre, format, and time period. One thing they all have in common, however, is that they were deliberately and coherently authored, published, distributed, and consumed. While such texts are important to study, there's been a link missing in the chain that connects personal stories to broader cultural narratives. (I'd even call it *an elephant in the room*, if I were inclined to mix clichés.) What is that missing link? Students have not yet engaged with the stories that are told—and endlessly retold—on social media.

This lesson directs students' attention to those stories. As I argued in the first half of this book, social media has shaped and tightened the connection between the personal and the cultural. We'd be remiss not to study the stories that circulate on social media—the micro stories, the incidental stories, the silly stories, the repetitive stories, even the seemingly incoherent stories— with the same level of rigor and close attention as we devoted to texts that were constructed in more traditional ways.

In this lesson, students explore a set of relatable memes. You'll want to choose memes that make use of a common meme format. Meme formats contain structural or semantic elements that make the meme a story. Because memes shift with the digital winds, it's impossible to be more specific about the memes you should choose. For this lesson, I've selected meme formats that are in wide use at the time of this writing, but you may want to swap them out for others.

The major work of this lesson is to analyze how character tropes and storylines show up in popular meme structures and to write two original memes: one that reinforces the cultural narrative and another that subverts it.

Opening and Invitation

In the opening activity, share three of the memes you've gathered. Invite students to rank each meme based on how relatable it is to their lives, using this ranking as a starting point for, hopefully, lively discussion. Then, guide students to do some quick, informal writing about whether they see evidence of character tropes or storylines in these memes.

Introduction of New Ideas

Share the full set of memes you've gathered with students and guide them to identify the common elements of the different formats. As students identify elements, chart them up, organizing them by type. For example, they might identify elements such as the following:

- **Captions** like POV, TFW, and "How It Started vs. How It's Going" are used to give the reader a way of interpreting an image or video
- **Music cues** like Stephen Sanchez's (2023) "Until I Found You" are used to mark a video as romantic
- **Dialogue frames** are used in "I'm a __. Of course, I __" memes to highlight both similarities and differences across human experience
- **Behavior labels** like Main Character Energy are used to evaluate certain behaviors or activities

Major Work of the Lesson, Part 1

Frame the major work of the lesson by explaining that something as simple—and unconsciously consumed—as a meme can do the work of telling larger cultural narratives. We must take a close look at the stories these memes tell about us and about the world we live in.

Students work in partners or small groups to re-examine the full set of memes you shared. This time, they focus on finding evidence of character tropes and storylines in these memes. "Evidence" might mean that a character trope or storyline is referenced directly or indirectly, that it's deployed to make the story of the meme coherent, or that it's somehow subverted. Support students by guiding them back to the specifics of their work from Lessons 2–3.

Bring students back together to share and discuss what they found.

Major Work of the Lesson, Part 2

In this second major activity, students create two of their own memes using the format of one of the memes they analyzed. The first meme should reinforce the character trope and/or storyline the element calls to mind. The second meme should subvert it.

Before they begin, share your own model memes, explain your thought process in developing them, highlight the format, and the character trope and/or storyline that's being reinforced and subverted. In the inset, I've provided a sample pair of memes, using the "also no" meme format. In this format, the implied speaker of the meme asks themselves a series of questions to which a reader would anticipate an affirmative answer. The speaker answers "no" to the first question and then "also no" to the subsequent questions, undercutting the hopefulness of the questions' framing. For example, one unattributed example posted on user Ashley Cordes's (n.d.) Pinterest account reads: "Am I a good person? No. But do I try to be better every single day? Also no."

Character Trope
Hapless, middle-aged woman who still doesn't have her life together

Meme Format
Also No

Reinforcing Character Trope
Do I have this whole adulting thing down?
No.
But do I try to accomplish at least one small task every day?
Also No.
But am I at least staying hydrated?
Again, No.

Subverting Character Trope
Do I have this whole adulting thing down?
Yeah, why do you ask?

Closing and Reflection

Students share the memes they created in small groups. If time permits, students can take feedback and recommendations from their small groups to revise and finalize them. Then, select a couple of memes from the class, display them without commentary from the author, and invite the rest of the class to analyze the character tropes and/or storylines present and determine if they're being reinforced or subverted.

Remixes

Teach this lesson as a standalone lesson in a unit about any current topic, curating the example memes and meme structures to relate to the topic of the unit. This would work especially well for a social studies unit. For example, in a unit about US presidential elections, select memes that relate to the current campaigns and elections. In a unit about capitalism as an economic system, select memes that relate to consumerism.

Embed ideas from this lesson into other lessons by having students create their own memes about a topic to develop or demonstrate their understanding of a topic.

Final Note: So What?

In July 2024, I taught an early draft of these lessons to a class of rising high school seniors. At first, I felt encouraged by the outcome of my instruction. The lessons went exactly as I'd envisioned them. My students were quick to pick up on the *storyline, character trope,* and *probable story* concepts, adept at finding and analyzing the cultural narratives hiding out in the silliest of memes, and even game to try the storytelling speed dating activity (which, I admit, is a dicey proposition for teens!).

Upon further reflection, though, I realized that, in my instruction, I'd missed something big: *so what? So what* if a short film like *One Small Step* (Pontillas & Chesworth, 2018) is built around a storyline, if there wasn't, so to speak, a dry eye in the house when we watched it? *So what* if teen movies deploy character tropes as perhaps a lazy narrative shorthand when that very device is what propels the film past the exposition and directly into the action?

I've since updated the lessons by incorporating discussion questions meant to move students into discussions of *so what?* But, if you leave some breathing room in your instruction, the young people will inevitably find this question on their own. If you let them, they'll be the ones to wonder, discuss, and debate how character tropes and storylines shape our view of ourselves and the world and whether they ultimately empower or disempower us.

When they do, it'll be important to remember that *so what?* is a question, not an answer. Critical engagement is not about demolishing a text through critical analysis of its hegemonic messaging and arriving at an enlightened view of its nefarious semiosis. It's about seeing texts as *texts* and about approaching them with self-awareness and intentional thought. You can't necessarily teach critical engagement, but you can give young people the opportunity to lead themselves there.

References

Barillaro, A. (Director). (2016). *Piper* [Film]. Pixar Animation Studios.

Cohen, J. (2024, May 2). She wanted a Brooklyn one-bedroom for less than $500,000, but where? *The New York Times*. www.nytimes.com/interactive/2024/05/02/realestate/brooklyn-one-bedroom-home-sale.html

Cordes, A. (n.d.). Also, no [Post]. Pinterest. www.pinterest.com/pin/149181806387370464/

Curtis, R. (Producer), & Michell, R. (Director). (1999). *Notting Hill* [Film]. Universal Pictures.

Frank, A. (2012). *Letter stories breathe: A socio-narratology*. The University of Chicago Press.

Glass, I. (Host). (1995–present). *This American life* [Audio podcast]. Chicago Public Media.

Heckerling, A. (Producer & Director). (1995). *Clueless* [Film]. Paramount Pictures.

Hughes, J. (Producer & Director). (1985). *The breakfast club* [Film]. Universal Pictures.

Jayne, S., & Perez, A. (Directors). (2024). *Mean girls* [Film]. Paramount Pictures.

Jenkins, B. [@BarryJenkins]. (2018, January 3). *In other news, the woman next to me is watching NOTTING HILL* [Post]. X. https://x.com/BarryJenkins/status/948711536415199233

Murphy, R. (Producer). (2009–2015). *Glee*. 20th Century Fox Television.

NASA. (1969). *Buzz Aldrin on the Moon with American flag* [Photograph]. NASA Images. www.nasa.gov/multimedia/imagegallery/image_feature_1003.html

Obama, B. H. (2004, July 27). *Keynote address at the Democratic National Convention*. Boston, MA. www.presidency.ucsb.edu/documents/keynote-address-the-2004-democratic-national-convention

Paskin, W. (Host). (2023). The recorder, limos, and "baby on board" signs [Audio podcast episode]. In *Decoder ring*. Slate.

Pontillas, B., & Chesworth, A. (Directors). (2018). *One small step* [Film]. TAIKO Studios.

Rodrigo, O. (2021). Driver's license [Song]. On *Sour*. Geffen Records.

Sanchez, S. (2023). Until I found you [Song]. Republic Records.

Søndergaard, D. M. (2002). Poststructuralist approaches to empirical analysis. *International Journal of Qualitative Studies in Education*, *15*(2), 187–204.

Star, D. (Producer). (1998–2004). *Sex and the city*. HBO.

White, R. (2008). *You belong with me* [Music video]. YouTube. www.youtube.com/watch?v=VuNIsY6JdUw

6

Autoethnography

The Self in Culture, Culture in the Self

In the first half of this book, I told a trio stories about my pop culture attachments. There was the one where I wrote a send-up of "Motownphilly" (Austin et al., 1991) called "Rainforest Feelin'" for a middle school science project; the one where I chronicled my every elder Millennial reaction to the *Sex and the City* (Star, 1998–2004) reboot on social media; and the one where I found myself wearing hand-made beaded friendship bracelets in middle age. These are stories about cultural objects—a song, a series, a podcast, a movie—and they're also stories about me. My pop culture attachments both reflect and reinforce my cultural identities and my individuality. And these stories, of course, are about culture itself: about the practices, values, beliefs, symbols, and objects that define a certain social milieu and shape the people who inhabit it.

These stories are my take on autoethnography. Autoethnography is a research genre in which the researcher examines their own personal experience in relation to the culture in which that experience unfolds (Ellis, 2004). As I think of it,

DOI: 10.4324/9781032667027-9

autoethnography is both a process and a product. As a process, it involves putting ourselves in active dialogue with the cultures we inhabit (and that inhabit us), examining the live, reciprocal connection between self and world.

Through this examination, we deepen our understanding of both who we are as unique selves and how we're shaped by what we see, read, and consume out in the world and, needless to say, on our devices. As a product, autoethnography is an expression of this deeper understanding, an artifact of active, critical, and strategic engagement with culture. It can serve as an example to others of what that engagement can be, what can be made of it, and how it can help us navigate the world with creativity and pluck. In the book-length autoethnography *My Life with Things: The Consumer Diaries*, for example, Elizabeth Chin (2016) examines her relationship with the consumer goods among which she lives her life. The book is organized into reflective vignettes about everyday items—shoes, window shades, napkins—and offers meditations on the larger social meanings of the items, her attachments to them, and consumption itself.

While autoethnography proper is a qualitative research genre, we can see the spirit of autoethnography everywhere, if only we widen our aperture. I see it in the viral dances discussed in Chapter 1, the critical memes discussed in Chapter 2, and the dark academia montages discussed in Chapter 3. I also see it in memoirs like Chef Gabrielle Hamilton's (2011) *Blood, Bones & Butter*, parts of which recount her relationship to the New York City restaurant scene in the 1980s and 90s, and Carmen Maria Machado's (2019) *In the Dream House*, in which the author finds herself contending with cultural representations of gender and sexuality. I see it in Ayad Akhtar's (2020) *Homeland Elegies*, a work of autofiction and a "staging and curation of the self" (as quoted in Schwartz, 2020) as a character confronting the racism and Islamophobia of post-9/11 America. I see it in Jamaica Kincaid's (1995) personal narrative "Putting Myself Together," an account of what she bought, ate, and wore as a young person in New York—and how she assembled an identity and a life for herself out of those details.

I even see autoethnography in poems like Ocean Vuong's (2022) "Amazon History of a Former Nail Salon Worker," which, as the title suggests, purports to reproduce the Amazon orders of a former nail salon worker as she dies of cancer; in opinion essays like Connie Wang's (2022) *New York Times* piece "Generation Connie," a chronicle of the distinctively Chinese-American Millennial experience of being named Connie; in some of the more thoughtful entries in human interest columns like *New York Magazine*'s "What I Can't Live Without" (2004–present) which offers notable figures' round-ups of the consumer goods they're fond of; and in visual art, like artist Cindy Sherman's (2024) self-titled exhibition of warped self-portraits that call to mind the ubiquitous practice of digitally manipulating one's likeness online.

What these examples have in common is that they show a self contending with the world, a self trying to figure out how to do it and what to make of it. These autoethnographers, so to speak, have put themselves through a process of noticing, reflecting, and making meaning. The autoethnographies that have resulted may or may not describe our own relationships to cultural objects, but they do serve as models of how to actively, critically, and strategically engage with culture.

Finding Mentors: Refashioning the Self

Let's take a closer look at one autoethnography-adjacent text: Hua Hsu's (2022) memoir *Stay True*. Hsu writes about his experience as a second-generation Taiwanese-American teen in California, learning what it means to be an American. He writes, "[Y]ou could refashion yourself a churchgoer, a pizza lover, an aficionado of classical music or Bob Dylan, a fan of the Dallas Cowboys because everyone in the neighborhood seemed to be one" (p. 18). The process of coming into one's American-ness, to Hsu, is one of "matriculating into a world of abundance" (p. 35).

Hsu settled on the kind of American he wanted to be when he discovered the song "Smells Like Teen Spirit" off Nirvana's

1991 album *Nevermind*. He was 13, and his appreciation of the song was largely derived from his sense that he had chosen it on his own—that he had "happened upon a secret before everyone else" (2022, p. 25). It was the process of choosing, the quality of "erudite discernment" (p. 27), that was for Hsu so exhilarating, so addictive. Loving "Smells Like Teen Spirit" is how Hsu figured out the kind of American—and the kind of person—he wanted to become. It allowed him to try on a new identity (critic, snob) and cultivate the pose and sensibility of that identity: in his words, "modest and small, sensitive and sarcastic, skeptical yet secretly passionate" (p. 26).

Of course, we know how the story ends. One day, to Hsu's dismay, everyone at school was wearing Nirvana t-shirts and singing "Smells Like Teen Spirit"—incorrectly, he notes—in biology. He liked Nirvana because he saw the band as occupying a fringe territory in American pop culture and, to Hsu, "the fringe territories were infinite" (2022, p. 26). When it turned out that everyone at school was into Nirvana, he had to face the fact that the infinite fringes are susceptible to being subsumed by the mainstream at any moment. (He doesn't say what he's made of fact that, today, 30-odd years later, Nirvana t-shirts have been absorbed into what Gen Z considers preppy style [Stankorb, 2023].)

Still, Hsu proved to be quite an active consumer of pop culture. He began publishing a music zine as "a way to find a tribe" (p. 26)—as well as to get free CDs from bands and record labels. He writes, "Making my zine was a way of sketching the outlines of a new self, writing a new personality into being. I was convinced that I could rearrange these piles of photocopied images, short essays, and bits of cut-up paper into a version of myself that felt real and true" (p. 26). Hsu's phrasing here echoes Kincaid's (1995) title "putting myself together." The notion that we fashion our identities from bits and fragments of culture is a motif I've noted across several autoethnographies I've studied.

What can we learn from Hsu's example? First, autoethnographies don't tend to be broad and comprehensive.

When we examine ourselves in relation to culture, we get the most intellectual and creative purchase when we start with a single cultural object we care about. Complexity and significance live in the specifics. Hsu started with one song, "Smells Like Teen Spirit," and then widened the scope of his reflection to include the album *Nevermind* and the genre of alternative music.

Second, the overarching purpose of autoethnography is to highlight the reciprocal relationships between the autoethnographer, the selected cultural object, and the broader culture. Showing these relationships in their fullness requires the autoethnographer to move in and out of the story of the object, taking both an endostory and an exostory stance (see Chapters 1 and 4). The autoethnographer both analyzes the elements of the object under study, examining how it was put together for a certain effect, and also narrates how they engage with it, the feelings it stirs up, the places to which it transports them. Autoethnography is neither ode nor critical analysis, though it may contain elements of both.

Third, a compelling autoethnography makes moves. Note how, in Hsu's chapter, there's a sense of movement and change. First, as he stumbled upon the song, he's invigorated by his perception of newness. That feeling brings about a sense that his appreciation of the song sets him apart from his peers. And so he begins to cultivate what he thinks of as coolness by way of erudite discernment. And then he really starts taking action: he creates a zine that both reflects and encourages his newfound sense of himself. Later in the chapter, Hsu describes how he and his father make sense of Cobain's 1994 death via an exchange of letters about creativity, societal pressure, and the contradictions between meaning and reality (p. 31). Hsu doesn't just capture a single moment of experience with the song. He captures ongoing engagement with it and shows how his understanding of the song, of American culture, and of himself shifts with new revelations, experiences, and choices. And, importantly, Hsu's narrative suggests that there's no finality. His relationship to the song and his understanding of that relationship continue to unfold.

Lessons on Autoethnography

The lessons in this chapter take young people through the process of composing a multimodal autoethnography. The lessons highlight the value of both the process and the product of autoethnography. The process of autoethnography involves identifying the cultural objects that matter to us and reflecting on how our personal relationship with the broader culture is exemplified, or shaped, or intensified, or complicated by these objects. The hope is that, through this process, students develop greater self-awareness and intentionality both in their storytelling and in the ways they choose to engage in the culture.

The lessons begin with an immersion in the autoethnography genre. This immersion allows students to extrapolate the key features of the genre and the benefits of engaging in the autoethnography process. On a practical level, the lessons offer multimodal composition tools and techniques, as well as time to plan, draft, workshop, and publish their multimodal autoethnographies.

Lesson 1: Exploring the Autoethnography Genre

The purpose of this multiday lesson is to immerse students in the genre of autoethnography. Autoethnography is the process of examining personal experience as it relates to culture, and the product we create to express what we discover.

In the lesson, students explore the genre in three stages, beginning with true autoethnographies and spiraling outward toward texts that can be more loosely defined as examples of autoethnography.

♦ First, they explore true autoethnographies drawn from peer-reviewed academic sources. These are, in other words, autoethnographies that call themselves *autoethnographies*

♦ Second, they explore written texts that, explicitly or implicitly, share the purposes and features of the genre. These might include poems, excerpts of memoirs, personal

> narratives, personal essays, or historical sources like speeches and letters
- ◆ Finally, they explore multimodal autoethnographies. These can be curated from a variety of online and print sources and might include slam poetry or other dramatic performances or graphic novels. They can even include everyday texts like memes and social media content

The most important way to prepare for this lesson is to curate these three sets of autoethnographies. You'll want to select examples that represent a diversity of experiences, cultures, genres, and formats. By immersing students in a wide range of examples, you'll nudge them toward a deep conceptual understanding of the genre, and you'll demonstrate that all identities, cultures, and relationships with culture are valued and worthy of examination and expression.

The major work of this lesson is to explore the genre. In doing so, students come to recognize and appreciate the benefits of the autoethnography process, understand the purposes of autoethnography products, and discern the types of content common to autoethnographies.

Opening and Invitation

Invite students to look through their phones or their belongings to identify one digital or physical object that someone else created that matters a lot to them. This might be a snippet of social media content, a game, an app, a song, an article of clothing or accessory, a book—or truly anything else, as long as it's something that someone else created. Students discuss why this object matters to them with a partner.

Launch this sequence of lessons by introducing the genre of autoethnography, highlighting the following points:

- ◆ Ethnography is a type of research that describes people and their cultures
- ◆ *Auto* means *self*, so *auto*ethnography is an examination of our own experiences as they relate to our cultures

- Autoethnography is about the process of examining ourselves and our lives, and it's also about the way we express what we've discovered to others
- In this sequence of lessons, we'll go through the process of examining our personal experiences as they relate to our cultures, and we'll create a product that expresses what we've discovered
- The product we create will be multimodal, which means it will include a combination of written, oral, visual, and auditory elements

Major Work of the Lesson

Invite students to explore three sets of autoethnographies over several days of instruction. Begin with true autoethnographies and then spiral outward toward texts that can be more loosely defined as examples of autoethnography. You might even invite students to find their own examples of autoethnography out in the digital wild to share with the class. For each set of autoethnographies, guide students to interpret the benefits the author might have experienced engaging in the autoethnography process, their purpose in creating the text and sharing it with others, and the specific content of each. Table 6.1 offers an overview of the types of autoethnography to include in each set.

Closing and Reflection

Students synthesize what they've learned about autoethnography in discussion and writing. Invite students to describe in their own words the benefits of the autoethnography process and the purposes of the autoethnography product; compare and contrast the content presented in two different autoethnographies that they studied; brainstorm examples of cultural objects or texts that they could use as the focus of their own autoethnographies and explain why those would be productive areas of focus.

Conclude the lesson by sharing the Autoethnography Project Rubric (Figure 6.1).

TABLE 6.1 Description and types of autoethnographies for exploration; intended outcomes of exploring each set.

Description	Types	Outcomes
Set 1: True Autoethnographies		
True research autoethnographies gathered from peer-reviewed academic sources	Book-length autoethnographies and journal articles	By the end of students' exploration of this first set of autoethnographies, students should understand: ◆ **Benefits:** The process of autoethnography helps the autoethnographer understand themselves and their cultures better. ◆ **Purposes:** Autoethnographies put the personal in relation to the cultural. The product of autoethnography can help the reader understand culture on a deeper level. ◆ **Content:** Autoethnographies might include personal anecdotes, descriptions of cultural texts, and commentary on the significance of those texts.
Set 2: Personal Writing		
Written texts that explore the relationship between the author and their culture	Poetry, memoir, personal narrative, autofiction, personal essay	By the end of students' exploration of this second set of autoethnographies, students should understand: ◆ **Purposes:** An autoethnography might seem like it's just about the individual person, but autoethnographies actually say something bigger about culture in general. Autoethnographies aren't trying to persuade the reader or make an argument; they're simply showcasing an example of a person relating to the culture. ◆ **Content:** Autoethnographies pull at something specific in the person's life—a specific time and place, a specific text or set of texts. Autoethnographies weave together story and commentary, external events and actions and internal thinking and feeling. Autoethnographies can take many different expressive forms.

(Continued)

TABLE 6.1 (Continued)

Description	Types	Outcomes
Set 3: Multimodal Writing		
Multimodal texts that explore the relationship between the author and their culture	Slam poetry, TED talks, dramatic performances, podcasts, graphic novels, meme carousels, social media content	By the end of students' exploration of this third set of autoethnographies, students should understand: ◆ **Content:** Autoethnographies can take many different expressive forms, including multimodal forms. Autoethnographers select their expressive tools wisely to highlight certain kinds of meanings and to speak to certain kinds of audiences.

Autoethnography Project Rubric

	Effective	Foundational	In Development
Cultural Product	The author selected a specific cultural object, developed its specificity, and vividly illustrated its personal significance.	The author selected a specific cultural object and has begun to develop its specificity and illustrate its personal significance.	The author selected a specific cultural object and presented relevant details about that object.
Relationships	The author meaningfully explored the multidirectional relationships among the object, the culture, and themself.	The author has begun to explore relationships among the object, the culture, and themself; some connections are not yet fully developed.	The author described at least one relationship among the object, the culture, and themself.
Movement	The author highlighted how and why their relationship to the object changed over time.	The author stated how their relationship to the object changed from one point in time to another.	The author mentioned that their relationship to the object has changed or will change but has not yet explored that change.
Multimodality	The author strategically employed multimodal elements to make their ideas clear and compelling.	The author incorporated multimodal elements to make their ideas clear.	The author has begun to incorporate multimodal elements, but these elements do not yet make their ideas clear.

FIGURE 6.1 Autoethnography project rubric.

Remixes

Teach this lesson as a standalone lesson by dropping it into a history unit. If your class is studying cultural elements of a historical period, find some primary sources that serve as autoethnographies. This lesson could also be dropped into a social studies unit that's meant to define *culture* itself. This lesson would help students understand that culture is not an externalized object, but a force people live with, within, and through every day.

Embed ideas from this lesson into other lessons. If you're studying a work of literature, see if there's another text by the same author that could serve as an autoethnography. Study that supplemental text to better understand both the author and their cultural context. For example, if you were studying Kincaid's (1983) "Girl," you could bring in an excerpt of "Putting Myself Together" (1995) and read the two texts against each other.

In a history lesson, use autoethnography as a conceptual process as a lens to understand a primary source document. Invite students to unpack the document to see what it reveals about how people of a time period experienced the culture of that time and place.

Lesson 2: Mining Personal Experience for Autoethnography

Now that students have learned about autoethnography as a process and a product, they're ready to begin work on their own autoethnography. In this lesson, students begin to plan their autoethnography. To do this, they reflect on their personal experience to identify possible topics. As they learned through the immersion, the topic of an autoethnography is narrow. Rather than capturing the whole of their cultural selves, autoethnographers focus their inquiry on a single cultural object or a specific time and place in their lives shaped by their engagements with culture. To support students in this work, model how to brainstorm possible topics and select the most promising among them.

The major work of this lesson is to identify two or three promising autoethnography topics.

Opening and Invitation

Students work collaboratively to review the mentor autoethnographies they explored in Lesson 1 and identify the topics. After this period of review, invite students to share the list of topics they identified and chart them for the whole class to see. Emphasize the range of topics addressed by these autoethnographers. If different students named different topics for the same autoethnography, encourage open discussion of why we might characterize the topic differently, depending on our own lenses as readers.

Introduction of New Ideas

Define *autoethnography topic* as your engagement with a specific cultural object that shaped you. Remind students of the full range of what counts as a cultural object: songs, films, TV shows, video games, books, social media content, clothing, toys, sports teams, and so forth. Model how to mine personal experience for autoethnography topics by brainstorming a list and then using guiding questions to select the most promising from that list. The inset shows an example of how this model might go.

I'm going to try two different strategies for brainstorming possible topics. My first strategy will be to think of a meaningful time in my life and then reflect on the aspects of culture that felt relevant to me then. The second strategy will be to think of a cultural object I really, really like—a song, a TV show, a social media account, a movie, a sports team, an item of clothing—and then reflect on why I like it so much.

When I think of meaningful times in my life, here's what comes to mind:

1. Being in middle school when I was starting to be exposed to lots of new music and new fashion, and everything felt fresh and exciting
2. When I first became a teacher, and I was learning about the pop culture my students were into and trying to incorporate it into my teaching
3. My life right now—especially as I've gotten really into learning about how clothes are made by reading about the topic and learning to sew and knit myself

Now, let me try the second strategy, which is to just think of cultural objects I like and then reflect on why I like them so much. Here's what comes to mind:

4. I love the sweater my mom got me as a gift when I was in college. It makes me feel connected to her and to the memory of getting it for the first time
5. I love the Taylor Swift song "Cruel Summer" (Swift et al., 2019). I've been listening to it on repeat. I always liked it, but I started really loving it when I found out how much my niece Perrine loves it, and we started singing it together
6. I love the TV show *The Bear*. I love the way the characters do their jobs. They take so much pride in what they do and what they make. I relate to that because I feel like a "maker." I always want to make things beautiful and inspiring for other people

Now that I've brainstormed this list of possible topics, I want to narrow it down to two or three that I think would make for a meaningful autoethnography. I can narrow it down by asking myself:

◆ Which topics feel most **salient** to me? Which speak to the core of who I am as a person?

◆ Which topics feel most **undecided** to me? Are there topics I don't fully understand the meaning of? Topics that bring up a feeling of tension in me? Topics I haven't quite figured out yet?

When I ask myself which feel most salient to me—which speak to the core of who I am—I have to say 1 and 6. I know middle school was a long time ago, but for some reason I still think about that time of my life! Maybe it's because that's when my tastes were formed. And 6 feels relevant because it's all about something very, very central to me, which is the idea that I'm a "maker." My friend Sayuri recently described me that way, and that's when I realized that that's a big part of how I approach life.

When I ask myself which feels most undecided to me, I have to say it's 5. It's such an unusual thing to feel just okay about a song and then, all of a sudden, you can't stop listening to it! There must be some deeper meaning there, but I'm not sure what it is. So the three topics I'm considering now are 1, 5, and 6.

Major Work of the Lesson

Students work independently to brainstorm a possible list of autoethnography topics using the two strategies you demonstrated (or any other strategies they devised!). After a brainstorming period, students talk out their possible topics with a partner, using the guiding questions: Which topics feel most salient? Which topics feel most undecided? By the end of this part of the lesson, students should have identified two or three possible autoethnography topics.

Closing and Reflection

Bring the class back together and invite students to reflect on the process of mining their personal experience:

◆ Was it easier to brainstorm the list of topics or to narrow down the list of topics? Why?

◆ When you were making your decisions, did you use your mind to think it out, or did you go with your gut?

◆ Do you feel confident in the two or three possible topics you've found? How do you know those will be meaningful topics for you to explore?

Remixes

Teach this lesson as a standalone lesson: This could be incorporated into a unit on personal narrative or memoir writing (or if they're working on college essays, for example). Teach this as a lesson about generating ideas, emphasizing the very transferable principle that, in the writing process, you've got to entertain lots of possible ideas before choosing one. You don't want to commit too early to an idea that's not going to sustain you through the process.

Embed ideas from this lesson into other lessons: At its core, this lesson is about how we as individuals relate to culture. The ideas from this lesson can be embedded in social studies lessons about *culture* as a concept. Use the reflective questions as an opening or warm-up to help students understand what culture is to them before defining the term more broadly.

Lesson 3: Understanding Personal Experience in Relation to Culture

This lesson asks students to engage in the most important intellectual work of the autoethnography project: examining how the *personal*—identities, experiences, values, and beliefs—relates to the *cultural*—the products, texts and milieus within and against which the personal unfolds. In this lesson, students select their final autoethnography topic and develop *what* they want to say. In the lesson that follows, they decide *how* they want to say it.

To develop what they want to say, students conceptually map the relationship between the personal and the cultural. They reflect on what the personal elements of their topic help them understand about the culture, and what the cultural elements help them understand about themselves. In doing this work, they might find it helpful to notice if and when they take an endostory stance or an exostory stance in relation to their topic.

The major work of this lesson is to conceptually map how the personal relates to the cultural in our lives and, in turn, in our autoethnographies.

Opening and Invitation

Share an excerpt of one of the autoethnographies from Lesson 1. The excerpt should showcase the relationship between the personal and the cultural. Invite students to discuss this relationship and chart their ideas. You might ask:

◆ What is *personal* here? What concerns the individual person?

◆ What is *cultural* here? What concerns the bigger culture the author is a part of?

◆ What do the *personal* elements help this autoethnographer understand about the culture?

◆ What do the *cultural* elements help this autoethnographer understand about themselves as a person and their experiences?

Then, invite students to reflect in writing on the possible autoethnography topics they generated in the previous lesson, select one topic, and simply list out the personal and cultural elements involved.

Introduction of New Ideas

Frame the work students will do in this lesson as autoethnographers, inviting them to recall that autoethnography is both a process and a product. Emphasize that we want to go beyond simply *including* the personal and the cultural. We want to engage in a reflective process that helps us understand how the personal and the cultural relate to each other. We'll use a conceptual map to make this thinking concrete. Preview the menu of conceptual map templates students can use to do this (see Figures 6.2, 6.3, and 6.4).

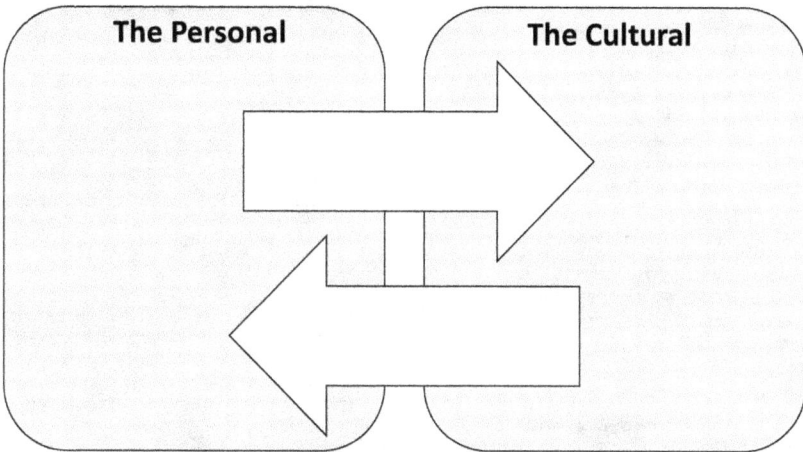

FIGURE 6.2 Personal-cultural connections template 1.

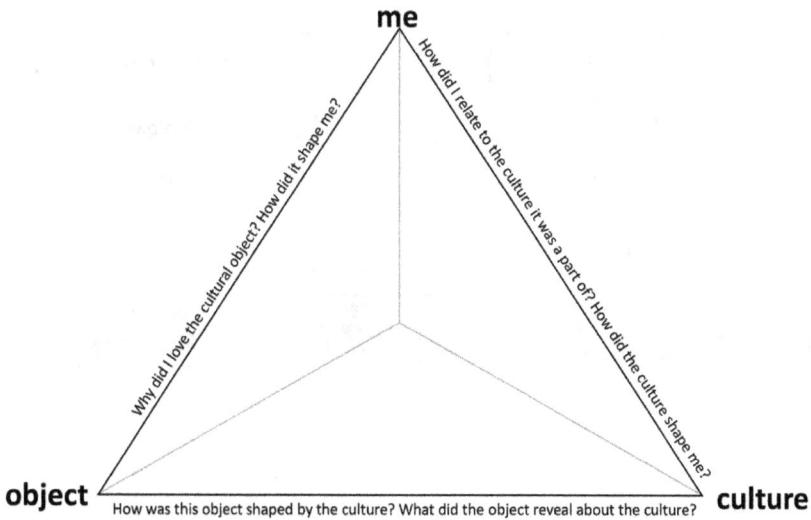

FIGURE 6.3 Personal-cultural connections template 2.

Major Work of the Lesson

Present an example of your own conceptual map of how the personal and the cultural relate and explain how you used the guiding questions to understand this relationship:

♦ What do the *personal* elements help me understand about the culture?

♦ What do the *cultural* elements help me understand about myself and my experiences?

What is a cultural object that is meaningful to you?	
Why is the object meaningful to you?	
What has the object revealed to you about yourself?	
How does this object fit in—or not fit in—with the larger culture?	
How do you fit in—or not fit in—with the larger culture?	
What do you say about the object?	
What does the object say about you?	

FIGURE 6.4 Personal-cultural connections template 3.

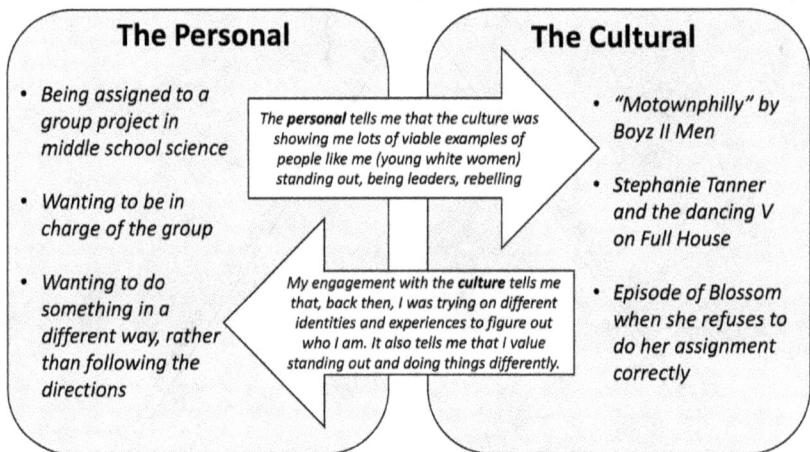

The Personal

- Being assigned to a group project in middle school science

- Wanting to be in charge of the group

- Wanting to do something in a different way, rather than following the directions

*The **personal** tells me that the culture was showing me lots of viable examples of people like me (young white women) standing out, being leaders, rebelling*

*My engagement with the **culture** tells me that, back then, I was trying on different identities and experiences to figure out who I am. It also tells me that I value standing out and doing things differently.*

The Cultural

- *"Motownphilly" by Boyz II Men*

- *Stephanie Tanner and the dancing V on Full House*

- *Episode of Blossom when she refuses to do her assignment correctly*

FIGURE 6.5 Model of conceptual map of personal-cultural connections.

Figure 6.5 shows an example of a conceptual map about my cultural engagements in middle school. I've included personal details (being assigned to a group project, wanting to be in charge, wanting to do something in a different way) and cultural details ("Motownphilly," Stephanie Tanner's dance scene in *Full House*, and Blossom's refusal to follow directions).

Emphasize that students can choose one of the given templates for their conceptual maps, adapt or modify one, or create one of their own. The overall purpose is for us to deepen our understanding of the relationship between the personal and the cultural and then to find a way to make that deeper understanding concrete.

Students work independently to reflect on and conceptually map the relationship between the personal and the cultural. After an initial period of independent work, invite students to talk through their responses to the guiding questions with a partner to further develop their thinking. Students can support each other by proposing other possible connections between the personal and the cultural.

To nudge students into deeper understandings, prompt them to consider how the relationship between the personal and cultural may have changed over time or how the relationship looks different from an endostory or an exostory perspective. You may want to do this in one-on-one conferences with individual students or as a whole-class work pause.

Closing and Reflection

Bring the class back together and invite students to reflect on the process of conceptually mapping the relationship between the personal and the cultural. You might ask:

- ◆ Was it easier for you to understand what the personal says about the cultural or what the cultural says about the personal? Why?
- ◆ When you thought about the cultural object you selected, did you find yourself taking an endostory reading stance, an exostory reading stance, or both? How did those stances help you connect the personal and the cultural?

Remixes

Teach this lesson as a standalone lesson: Like Lesson 2, this lesson could be incorporated into a unit on personal narrative, memoir, or college essay writing. Some students writing in these genres will develop themes and messages that are relevant only to them. Mapping out the connection between the personal and the cultural could help them develop themes and messages of broader consequence and resonance for readers.

Embed ideas from this lesson into other lessons: The idea that the personal and the cultural are interconnected could be embedded in a history lesson about the cultural factors of a historical time period. Students could study some primary source accounts of cultural engagement from the time period and conceptually map how the author makes connections between the personal and the cultural.

In an ELA lesson, students can conceptually map this relationship for a character in a book, considering how elements of the character's identity, experiences, values, and beliefs relate to the culture they inhabit.

Lesson 4: Multimodal Tools for Autoethnography

The purpose of this multiday lesson is to move students toward creating their final autoethnography products. In the previous lessons, they developed the *content* of their autoethnography: what they want to say about themselves in relation to culture. In this lesson, they will decide on the *genre* and *format* of the product. Once they've made this decision, they'll be ready to make a project plan that lays out when they will draft each part, what tools they'll need, and whom they could ask for support.

The way you facilitate this lesson and customize the project planning template will depend on a handful of contextual factors. For example, do you plan to have students work on their autoethnography products mostly in class or mostly at home? What kinds of tools will they have available to them in the classroom and/or at home? How wide of a range of options can you feasibly support? The lesson below assumes the fullest range of options with unlimited access to the necessary tools, but, as you plan to teach this lesson, keep these contextual factors in mind.

The major work of the first day of this lesson is to select a genre and format for their final autoethnography product and create a project plan. The major work from there is to go about composing their autoethnography product.

Opening and Invitation

Invite students to review the mentor autoethnographies they examined in Lesson 1—especially the multimodal examples in the third set. Students discuss how the modes used in these texts helped the authors express their ideas. Consider using the following questions to guide this discussion:

◆ What do the visual elements help us understand?
◆ What do the verbal/language elements help us understand?
◆ What do the auditory/sound elements help us understand?
◆ Why might this author have chosen to make a [genre/ format] rather than a simple written text?

Preview the work of this lesson: we'll decide on the best genre and format to express the ideas we developed in the previous lessons.

Introduction of New Ideas, Part 1

To support students in choosing a genre and format for their autoethnography, introduce the concept of *modal affordance*. Explain that a *mode* is a way of communicating meaning. We categorize modes as linguistic, visual, auditory, gestural, spatial, and tactile.

Define *modal affordance*: what is possible to express, represent, and communicate in a particular mode. Connect this definition to the discussion at the top of the lesson. Explain that, when evaluating modal affordances, it can be helpful to consider how time and space work in each mode. Highlight these principles:

◆ We can use different modes to guide our readers' attention in different ways.
◆ If we want to control the order in which readers receive ideas and information, we can choose a mode that uses time. Audio, video, and printed text put ideas and information in a specific order for readers to take in.

◆ If we want to control how readers envision and understand the relationships between different elements, we
can choose a mode that uses space. Visual modes—
including photos, drawings, infographics, diagrams,
maps, and more—help us put a picture in our readers'
minds and make our ideas and the connections between
our ideas feel more real and concrete.

Illustrate these principles using some of the familiar examples
students have already studied. Review the menu of possible
genres and formats from which students can choose (Table 6.2).
Students should consider the modes involved in their selected
genre and format and the materials and tech required. Highlight
the genre and format you selected and why, based on your analysis of the modal affordances.

Major Work of the Lesson, Part 1

Students review the menu of options, evaluate the modal
affordances of the options, and select their preferred genre
and format. Encourage students to entertain multiple possible
options and discuss possibilities with a partner before selecting
one. Students document their choices at the top of their project
planning template (Figure 6.6).

Introduction of New Ideas, Part 2

Bring the class back together to preview the rest of the project
planning template and share an example of your own complete
project plan. The project plan should include:

◆ A break-down of the sections of the autoethnography
◆ The date(s) on which the student will draft each section
◆ The tasks they'll need to complete to draft each section
◆ The tools and resources needed to complete the tasks
◆ The people who can support with the tasks

Major Work of the Lesson, Part 2

Students work independently to create a project plan, using the
project planning template. Circulate and encourage students to

TABLE 6.2 A menu of possible autoethnography genres and formats, their modes, and the materials and tech tools needed to create them.

Autoethnography Genres, Formats, and Modes

Genre	Format	Modes	Materials and Tech
Screencast	Video	Linguistic, visual, auditory, spatial	◆ Computer with presentation software (PowerPoint, Google Slides, Canva) ◆ Screen recording software (QuickTime, Photo Booth, Screencastify)
Short film	Video	Linguistic, visual, auditory, gestural	◆ Smartphone ◆ Computer with video editing software (iMovie, Filmora)
Photovoice essay	Video	Linguistic, visual, auditory	◆ Smartphone with camera ◆ Voice recording app or software (Voice Memos, Voice Record Pro) ◆ Photo editor (Adobe Lightroom)
Song	Live performance, video, or audio	Linguistic, auditory, gestural	◆ Staff paper and/or songwriting software or app (e.g., Songcraft, BandLab, GarageBand) ◆ Smartphone with camera
Play, or one-person show	Live performance or video	Linguistic, visual, auditory, gestural	◆ Word processing software ◆ Smartphone with camera
Podcast	Audio	Linguistic, auditory	◆ Smartphone with voice recording app (Voice Memos, Voice Record Pro) ◆ Audio editing software
Infographic	Digital text	Linguistic, visual, spatial	◆ Computer with program that allows you to manipulate text/images (Microsoft PowerPoint, Adobe Photoshop, Canva)

(Continued)

TABLE 6.2 (Continued)

Autoethnography Genres, Formats, and Modes

Genre	Format	Modes	Materials and Tech
Website, blog, or newsletter	Digital text	Linguistic, visual, spatial	◆ Computer with account on website/blog platform (Squarespace, WordPress, Tumblr)
Graphic novel	Physical text	Linguistic, visual, spatial	◆ If drafting digitally, graphic design software (Adobe Spark, Canva) ◆ If drafting by hand, comic panel drafting paper and colored pencils, pens, or markers
Pamphlet	Physical text	Linguistic, visual, spatial	◆ Word processing software with pamphlet template
Poster	Physical text	Linguistic, visual, spatial	◆ Word processing software ◆ Graphic design software (Adobe Spark, Canva) ◆ Posterboard ◆ Pens, markers, scissors ◆ Colored paper for backgrounds and decorative elements
Art object	Physical object	To be determined by the student's vision and method	◆ To be determined by the student's vision and method

Project Planning Template

Autoethnography Genre and Format:				
Section	Date(s)	Drafting Tasks	Tools and Materials I'll Use	Support I'll Need

FIGURE 6.6 Project planning template.

refer to the information in the menu of options as they consider the tools and support they might need to complete each task.

Closing and Reflection
Bring the class back together and invite students to reflect on the project plan they created. Ask:

♦ Why did you choose the genre and format you chose? What makes you excited about creating that kind of autoethnography?

♦ What new skills might you learn as you create your autoethnography? Who or what can help you learn those skills?

♦ What challenges might come up as you work through your project plan? How will you address those challenges?

Ongoing Work
Over the next several days, students craft their autoethnographies, following the project plan they developed. Consider incorporating opportunities for students to receive one-on-one coaching and feedback from you. Lesson 5 offers ideas for peer workshops that would cap off this period of work.

Remixes
Teach this lesson as a standalone lesson in any project-based unit in which students develop a multimodal product. Students

can use the menu of genres and formats (Table 6.2) and project planning template (Figure 6.7) to make choices about their product and plan their work.

Embed ideas from this lesson into other lessons: The major idea of this lesson is project planning. Any time students are planning a project of any kind, engage students in a process of breaking down the tasks, timelining them, identifying the necessary tools, anticipating challenges and identifying people you could partner with for support.

Lesson 5: Autoethnography Workshop

This lesson follows a series of days of work on the autoethnography. By this point, students have created a near-final draft of their multimodal autoethnography product and are ready to revise, edit, and prepare it for publication. To prepare for this lesson, give some thought to how you want students to publish their autoethnographies. You might host a community event during which students can share, read from, and discuss their autoethnographies with small groups. You might also create a physical display that others in the school community can visit or even share their work on a school social media account. Whatever you decide, be sure to discuss with students how their work will be published so they can have specific readers and audiences in mind as they finalize their pieces.

In this lesson, students meet in small collaborative groups to workshop the drafts using a feedback protocol adapted from Matthew Salesses's (2021) *Craft in the Real World*. In this protocol, students use the Autoethnography Project Rubric (Figure 6.1) to focus their feedback on the most important elements of the genre: selecting a meaningful cultural object, showing the relationship between the personal and the cultural, and tracking the relationship through time.

To teach this lesson as written, students share their drafts with a small group (of three, ideally) in advance of this lesson so that students have time to engage with the draft and develop some preliminary feedback. Students should have already completed the first two steps of the protocol before this lesson begins.

The major work for this lesson is to workshop autoethnography drafts and make plans for revision and publication.

Before the Lesson

Introduce the workshop protocol (Table 6.3) and invite students to review the guidance for each step. Share an example of how

TABLE 6.3 Autoethnography workshop protocol.

Autoethnography Workshop Protocol

Step	Guidance
1. The author **submits a draft with writing notes** that describe their process, their intended audience, and the craft decisions they made while creating the product.	As you draft your writing notes, consider the questions: What was I trying to convey to my audience? What decisions did I make to try to convey that message?
2. Peers **develop a written description** of what they've read, addressing what it's about and the craft decisions that were made.	Describe your peer's work without evaluation or judgment. Simply try to capture what you take to be the author's intended message and the decisions they made to convey it.
3. During the workshop time, peers **take turns sharing their descriptions** of what they've read.	As you get ready to share, determine the order in which you'll share in advance. At this stage, stick to what you wrote. Simply read it aloud as the author listens and takes notes.
4. The author **responds to the descriptions and poses questions** to frame the discussion.	You might pose questions about what led your peers to their interpretations, or about which moves they felt most effectively conveyed your message. You might also ask clarifying questions.
5. The group **discusses the author's questions.**	This stage of the workshop is a more open-ended discussion of the author's questions. Anyone can jump in at any time.
6. Peers **propose possible revisions** by offering *what-ifs*.	At this stage, the open-ended discussion focuses in on specific possibilities for revision. The group asks, "What if . . .?" filling in possible steps the author could take.
7. The author **names two or three steps** they will take in their revision.	After listening to your peers' *what-ifs*, decide which specific steps you're ready to take next to revise your autoethnography.

you completed **Step 1: develop writing notes that describe your process, intended audience, and the craft decisions you made while creating the product**. Then, invite students to independently complete Step 1.

Create groups of three students and arrange for them to share their autoethnography drafts and writing notes with each other. Before the workshop, they'll review their group members' drafts, as well as your draft, and complete **Step 2: develop a written description of what you've read, addressing what it's about and the craft decisions that were made.**

Opening and Invitation

Review the steps of the workshop protocol including the first two steps, which they've already completed.

Review the Autoethnography Project Rubric (Figure 6.1). To practice applying the rubric to the written description of the product, select a previously studied autoethnography mentor text and invite students to develop and then share a short written description of the piece using the language of the rubric.

After this practice, students review the written feedback they've already prepared and annotate or update it to reflect the rubric criteria.

Introduction of New Ideas

Students practice the protocol by working through Steps 3–7 as a whole class, using your autoethnography draft. For the purposes of the practice, you can select a few students to share their descriptions in Step 3, rather than asking every student to share. You might also condense the discussion time.

Major Work of the Lesson

In their pre-assigned small groups, students workshop their autoethnography drafts by working through Steps 3–7 of the protocol. The student whose work is under discussion can use the Revision Plan Template to jot notes (Figure 6.7).

Revision Plan Template

Autoethnography Workshop Notes	Revision Step	What and Why?	How and When?

FIGURE 6.7 Revision plan template.

Closing and Reflection

Students share the top revision they've decided to make to their autoethnography. Invite the class to discuss the publication plans for the autoethnography, including:

◆ Publication or event date
◆ Audiences who will be invited to attend and/or engage with autoethnographies
◆ Logistics of publication, including tools and resources needed

Remixes

Teach this lesson as a standalone lesson in any writing or project-based unit in which students develop a final product. The workshop protocol can be applied to a wide range of scenarios in which students compose a piece that demonstrates their thinking or understanding.

Final Note: To Be a Cultural Being

In school, young children are often asked to write personal narratives. One of the most common techniques for generating story ideas is to ask them to find an object among their belongings that holds special meaning for them. Maybe that object shows up in their final narrative, or maybe it doesn't. But at least when I've taught these lessons, the child's first step in planning their story is to pivot away from the object into something deeper about their identity or relationships. The story's not really about the cute emoji key chain on your backpack; it's about your relationship with your older sister who bought it for you. This kind of personal narrative writing creates an occasion for children to develop their writing skills, habits of mind, motivations, and storytelling instincts.

The lessons in this chapter start the same way—identifying an object that means something—but they ultimately ask young people to do something very different. These lessons ask young people to stay with the object, to examine it, to see what it might reveal about who we are as cultural beings. That's the intention and promise of writing autoethnography: the process helps us see ourselves as cultural beings, neither defined by culture nor able to stand fully apart from and outside of it.

It's a rigorous idea—one that doesn't mean much of anything in theory but means a whole lot in practice. After all, truly active, critical, and strategic engagement with culture isn't possible if we don't know where we stand, and how we stand, in relation to it.

References

Akhtar, A. (2020). *Homeland elegies: A novel*. Little, Brown and Company.

Austin, M., Bivins, M., Morris, N., & Stockman, S. (1991). Motownphilly [Song]. On *Cooleyhighharmony*. Motown Records.

Chin, E. (2016). *My life with things: The consumer diaries*. Duke University Press.

Ellis, C. (2004). *The ethnographic I: A methodological novel about autoethnography*. AltaMira Press.

Hamilton, G. (2011). *Blood, bones & butter: The inadvertent education of a reluctant chef*. Random House.

Hsu, H. (2022). *Stay true: A memoir*. Doubleday.

Kincaid, J. (1983). Girl. In J. Kincaid, *At the bottom of the river* (pp. 3–5). Farrar, Straus and Giroux.

Kincaid, J. (1995, February 12). Putting myself together. *The New Yorker.* www.newyorker.com/magazine/1995/02/20/putting-myself-together

Machado, C. M. (2019). *In the dream house.* Graywolf Press.

New York Magazine. (2004–present). What I can't live without [Column]. https://nymag.com/tags/what-i-can%27t-live-without/

Salesses, M. (2021). *Craft in the real world: Rethinking fiction writing and workshopping.* Catapult Books.

Schwartz, A. (2020, September 21). An American writer for an age of division. *The New Yorker.* www.newyorker.com/magazine/2020/09/21/an-american-writer-for-an-age-of-division

Sherman, C. (2024). *Cindy Sherman* [Exhibition]. Hauser & Wirth, New York.

Stankorb, S. (2023, October 6). No apologies. *Slate.* https://slate.com/human-interest/2023/10/nirvana-shirts-tiktok-trend-style-preppy-teens.html

Star, D. (Producer). (1998–2004). *Sex and the city* [TV series]. HBO.

Swift, T., Antonoff, J., & Clark, A. (2019). Cruel summer [Song]. On *Lover.* Republic Records.

Vuong, O. (2022). Amazon history of a former nail salon worker. In O. Vuong, *Time is a mother.* Penguin Press.

Wang, C. (2022, May 11). Generation Connie. *The New York Times.* www.nytimes.com/interactive/2023/05/11/opinion/connie-chung-named-after.html

Conclusion

Researching how young people engage with pop culture, I've felt myself tipping back and forth between two extremes of feeling. Some days, I'm disillusioned and distraught. The current state of pop culture seems dire. *Kids are addicted to their phones! They're anxious! They have no attention span! They do whatever they see on TikTok! We have to do something!* But other days, I'm awed by the humor, sensitivity, and ingenuity young people bring to their pop culture engagement.

On the bad days, I'm reminded of a scene from the first season of Mike White's (2021) series *White Lotus*. The Mossbacher family, seated for dinner at a luxury resort in Maui, argue, with unsettlingly quiet intensity, about the state of the world. A generational conflict is unfolding between Nicole, the CFO of a tech company, and her daughter Olivia. Olivia accuses Nicole of being complicit in economic exploitation; Nicole questions the sincerity of Olivia's progressive beliefs, given her willingness to enjoy the spoils of that exploitation.

Quinn, the younger son, who's been silent, breaks in: "What does it matter what we think? If we think the right things or the wrong things? We all do the same shit. We're all still parasites on the Earth."

On the bad days, I, like Quinn, fear that, in this cultural context, nothing about our inner lives—about who are—matters anymore. We've been flattened, our attention mined for profit. We scroll, we post, we let 45 minutes go by before we realize we've watched almost an entire movie in clips on TikTok. We pick up our phone, we pick up our phone, we pick up our phone. Whatever once made us unique has been washed away in a flood of *content*.

The good days are good, usually, because I'm with young people. Recently, I pestered a group of my students, rising high school seniors, to sit down with me over lunch and answer all my questions about online culture. They presented example after example of their individuality and savvy as consumers of culture, made case after case that they are active, critical, and strategic. They told me what they like and what they don't like, and why, and how they manipulate their algorithm to see what they want to see.

They weighed the pros and cons of different social media platforms (Instagram's algorithm is better, less chaotic, than TikTok's, but you can't post on Instagram every day unless you're a content creator). They disagreed about which streamers and content creators were worth watching, and which had sold out, and when, and why, and how their having sold out changed their content. They're discerning; they have taste. And they told me that, contrary to Millennial assumptions about them, they do still like watching whole TV shows and movies and listening to whole songs.

In *Inside*, comedian Bo Burnham's 2021 musical special, Burnham sends up the motifs of a white woman's Instagram: fuzzy socks, tiny pumpkins, latte foam art, quotes misattributed to Martin Luther King, dogs in flower crowns, and so forth. The march of clichés feels unrelenting, until it relents. Halfway through the song, the white woman character posts a photo of her mom, who died a decade earlier. The caption is earnest: she misses her mom, it's been hard to live without her, but she's doing well, she would be proud of her little girl. This interlude illustrates that, even in a sea of sameness, humanity finds a way to make itself known.

Of course, neither view—that the kids are doomed, that the kids are just fine—is correct on its own. I argue that our charge as educators is to see it both ways, to get used to that feeling of tipping back and forth.

References

Burnham, B. (Director). (2021). *Bo Burnham: Inside* [Film]. Netflix.
White, M. (Writer & Director). (2021). Recentering (Season 1, Episode 4) [TV series episode]. In *The White Lotus*. HBO.

For Product Safety Concerns and Information please contact our EU
representative GPSR@taylorandfrancis.com
Taylor & Francis Verlag GmbH, Kaufingerstraße 24, 80331 München, Germany